Knowing the author and watching h
she created this book was inspiring! The book is an
excellent overview of the utterly amazing energy
healing work she does. As a Nurse Practitioner, I
have experienced this healing firsthand, and her
book is very enlightening about aspects of healing
that never get discussed in a traditional office visit.
Highly recommend this book for people who want
more than a prescription, especially if you want to
empower yourself.

- Maureen, Healthcare practitioner

Marie is incredibly unique in this area of
knowledge. She enables you to really go inside
yourself to ask for answers. A fresh look at how we
can connect with our own intuition and really
connect with ourselves and the world around us. If
you are looking for answers to life's questions, you
may be surprised where the answers lie, and the
path you take to get them. This book helps you to
realize that the possibilities are endless.

- Dana, Specialty Car Creator

This book is a great read for anyone that wants a
better understanding and fresh perspective on life
energy. Marie will help you think "outside the box"
and focus on what is truly the "body within" all of
us! I highly recommend this book, ESPECIALLY to
anyone that works in the healing arts

- Deb, Massage Therapist

Marie Knoetig/Global Reality Publishing

BEDFORD, NEW HAMPSHIRE

Book Layout ©2015 BookDesignTemplates.com

Ordering Information:

www.amazon.com

www.marieknoetig.com

For Bulk Orders, please contact us directly at marieknoetig@gmail.com.

The Body Within/ Marie Knoetig. —Revised Edition.

ISBN 9780996603232

Marie Knoetig

THE BODY WITHIN

Who Are You Really?

Marie Knoetig

Global Reality Publishing

Disclaimer

I am introducing a new method, called *The Body Within.* I am not a medical doctor, and I do not practice medicine. My definition of healing is based on the energy field that connects us to the universe.

I don't prescribe medications, but as part of my practice do suggest healthcare options. I assist people in correcting energy imbalances in the different fields of their being to release negative energy. When the energy of the body is balanced, the body's natural energy heals itself.

All healing promoted in this book and my work is self-healing. I strongly recommend that clients continue to see their regular medical practitioners and use my work as a complement to their healing.

The methods and theories in this book have worked for me and my healing. They may or may not be right for you and your healing. You need to use your own judgment in exploring and using any exercises or techniques in this book.

If you are concerned about any health issue you may have, please see a qualified physician for guidance.

.

The individual case studies used in this book are true. However, names and descriptive details have been changed to protect the identities of those involved.

This book is dedicated to my brother, Steve.

Life has handed us many challenges. The one constant in my life has been that you have always had my back, and I have always had yours. The security you have afforded me through the years is the main reason I have become the strong woman I am today. I am forever grateful to have you in my life.

Love you!

Table of Contents

Interested In Learning More?

Visit <u>**MARIEKNOETIG.COM**</u> for

Free Meditations, EBooks, A Self Study Course, Private Sessions, and Upcoming Seminars!

The Body Within Healing Series

Preface

Do you suffer from chronic pain or illness, or are you just looking to regain total health and wellness to set the stage for aging gracefully?

There is so much information available to you, so many quick fix answers, so many drugs and so many supplements, but no real understanding of what your role is in accomplishing personal wellness. You listen to what your doctor says but sometimes it feels like it is not right or not enough. Then you go the holistic practitioner route; there is so much more information to process, so many supplements to take, it becomes overwhelming. Again, you feel like there should be something else, but you are not sure of what that something is. Next, you turn to books, speakers, and the internet. Why doesn't anyone agree? As soon as you read that something that might work, (and you're so relieved!) you find out that many articles to say it's good and just as many to say it's bad. Your only hope is to find a doctor or practitioner that will help you sort things out. This becomes difficult as I have found that very few practitioners can remain subjective to be of much assistance.

In my work, I find the biggest piece missing in medicine is that no matter what modality you choose: the drugs, the supplements seem to be the answer but there is so much more. You are so much more. You have innate knowledge to know how to heal yourself.

When you are diagnosed with a problem from a broken arm to cancer, what happens when you leave the office of your trusted practitioner and go home? There is so much down time for healing in between appointments. What is your role in healing besides doing what they said? Shouldn't you have your own piece in healing to add to the knowledge they have given you? Isn't healing more than just a pill, surgery, a prescribed exercise or diet, or supplements? There are so many things you can do to support your healing in conjunction with the medicine you choose. The more we learn what those things are, the more the tools keep emerging. The real beauty of this is sometimes those tools can get you to the point of not needing much of the medicine at all.

What you need to know is what to do when your body is out of sync or balance and under the stress of illness or everyday life. Do you really believe you were born helpless as far as healing and understanding your own body? Do you really need to wait for a professional to tell you what is best for you? It would seem we should already know, doesn't it? As amazing as humans are, somehow along our journey through Evolution we forgot how to tap into the part of us that knows us better than we know ourselves, better than anyone else knows us. I call that *The Body Within*.

The Body Within is the true essence of who you are. It knows how to show you how to heal your aches and pains, and to know if the treatments you are choosing are in your best interest. *The Body Within* knows to alert you to self-destructive behaviors that hurt your physical body. *The Body Within* can help guide you to make a sound decision on what medicine is best for you at the time you need it. *The Body Within* can guide you daily into making positive choices to heal your illness, pain, grief and many other issues that stress your bodies and inhibit healing. *The Body Within* can teach you to be more present and aware of your physical body and when it is off so you can correct the imbalances. *The Body Within* can help you rebalance yourself to your busy life, can help heal your illness, become healthy, strong and age graceful to enjoy your later years.

That is what this book is about. It's about you tapping into all the unlimited possibilities in yourself and your surroundings to help you become the healthiest, most balanced you! My goal for you is once you know yourself better, your medical choices become easier and more effective.

I will take you on a journey of personal case studies that range from illness to chronic pain, from birthing and dying and everything in between. I will show you how a medical practitioner does not prescribe healing. It isn't "the illness" or "the accident", and then a 6-8 weeks healing time. It's more than that—it depends on you and what you do during and after those weeks' end. The healing is a daily progression of who you are and how you want your quality of life to be from your birth to your death. Healing is very personal; it comes in many packages but mostly from you being aware and present with yourself to know what you feel like when you are healthy, so then you will have a strong sense when things aren't right with you. This Knowing puts you in the driver's seat, so when someone gives you advice regarding your health, you will have a clearer picture of whether it is right for you or not. You will become more aware of issues that cause you to become ill. You will understand how most illness come from living a life of chaos and learning to live a life of balance puts you back in the drivers' seat to greater health and wellness.

Take your time reading each case study and see if it relates to you or someone you know; look for the many tools I offer to help you connect to *The Body Within*. The more you connect, the more tools you will have to heal illness already present in your body, and even better, you will learn to be one step ahead of illness you might be creating. Take the time to get to know *The Body Within*, and then you are one step closer to total health.

Happy Reading!
Marie

Introduction

I'm a hands-on person, so I'm putting into words what would be much easier to explain if I were to work with you one on one. I feel very strongly that my message will not only help you, but it will help you help others around you as well. This is how *The Body Within* came to light. When someone is on my treatment table, I am able to tap into the life force energy of their body (their chi flow), the energy in all of us that connects us to the universe. As I do this, I can see or sense their energy anatomy and any blockages in their energy that might be inhibiting the person's healing. It could be physical or emotional imbalances in their life. On a more specific level, it could be imbalances in the muscular skeletal system and any dysfunctions that are keeping the body from healing.

What do I mean by this? When I look at an individual, I not only see them lying in front of me on the table. I see an energy imprint on their physical body along with other layers of energy. It's like someone puts a clear piece of plastic in front of their physical body and marks lines and spots on it to show where the dysfunction in the ti sue lies. Here's an example: You come in to see me because you have had right shoulder pain for two years with no recollection of an injury, and physical therapy or any advice the doctors have given you has not resolved the issue. I can see or sense these imprints energetically and, a lot of times, figure out what is causing the shoulder pain. Sometimes, I might sense the pain is caused by the opposite knee and a dysfunction in your gait (your manner of walking or running.)

Or it might be you had your appendix removed and I see or sense some of the scar tissue is now restricting you from fully lifting your arm from the midsection of your torso, which causes pressure on your shoulder joint. Or you might have had a torn ACL (ligament) repair in the opposite knee six or more years prior to the shoulder pain onset and this is what is the real source of your pain.

You see, every time you sustain an injury to your body, the body immediately puts up a wall of protection to protect the part of the body that has been injured to prevent further injury. This wall not only shuts down body movement in the area of the injury, but it also limits movement in other areas of the body that affect the injury, areas you may not even realize are related to the limitation or pain you are having. In time, as you heal the injury, you regain a good portion of movement back, but a lot of times you still have some dysfunction in the area of the injury or any areas of movement in the body that pull on the injury while healing. This is what I see energetically, the left-over debris, as I call it.

If you don't clean up and regain full function from a previous injury, it starts to create blockages in your energy imprint, as well as the fluid gate of your body. This can cause new injuries to heal slowly or improperly, and even aid in creating an injury due to what is called "cumulative trauma disorder." The fascinating part is everyone has lived their lives in a completely different manner, so one person's body does not have the same injuries or imprints as another person. Sometimes, to help a new injury heal, there is a pattern that an old injury or dysfunction creates that needs to be found. With my intuitive abilities, I can use energy as a tool. I can see or sense your energy imprint of past injuries to help you resolve the shoulder issue after you figure out what is slowing the healing of the shoulder. I am also able to sense in your physical body what might be fatiguing your body which would cause illness as well.

From there, I am self-taught in hands-on energy release of tissue restrictions. Using my intuition and my knowledge of how the body moves - from my training with exercise and my degree in Exercise Science. - I work with the individual to help facilitate the body in energetically releasing these restrictions and help the individual regain mobility back to the limited joints.

Then, I work with the individual to progress toward creating balance in their lives so they can start to work on self-healing this or any other physical issues. Each session is individualized, so when the client comes in, I am able to connect to their personal energy field, what I call *The Body Within*. Throughout this book, the many case studies will show the different ways I can connect to *The Body Within* to aid an individual in healing.

I believe *The Body Within* is the true essence of who you are. As soon as I connect with a client energetically, *The Body Within* of my client guides me through the endless possibilities in their healing. Sometimes during the session, I key in on the energetic blockages in the physical body, sometimes it's emotional, and sometimes I work with the energies that are creating an imbalance in the client's life. These could be stress, anger, sometimes negativity, or even grief. This can cause an imbalance in each person's energies. There are so many ways the body struggles to heal and working with these reasons and helping the client create balance aids the healing process. As I work with a client and connect with *The Body Within*, I help them connect deeper within themselves. The benefits of this established connection are limitless. Learning how to heal by connecting and looking inward not only serves you now but also as you age.

You might be thinking, "Does she consider herself a psychic or medium or someone like that?" I answer that with a definite "NO!" What I consider myself is a person who is sensitive to the subtle energies that we all are made of. Someone who has, through her own healing, tapped into a small piece of the endless possibilities we all are as humans. By being balanced in life and present with each client, along with the many skills I have acquired in my life, I am able to see what most of us miss happening around us daily. Being open and balanced has helped me become a facilitator for those who want to learn more about their own bodies and the life force energy that is us. In doing this, I can help the individual create healing for themselves. This book is written to help you get these skills for yourself.

This self-taught technique also aids in many other health issues such as autoimmune, arthritis, cancer, and so forth. Helping you with energy balancing and teaching you about your energy anatomy along with getting you to be more present in your body aids you in their everyday living. It also helps you in making choices and becoming more aware of the imbalances in energy around you, whether it's work, family, diet, rest, friends, or even outside energetic influences such as the news, weather, even events happening in the environment.

My goal in writing this book is to show you how you can interpret the energy anatomy of your body and how you can use it to self-heal your own body and life. How the choices you make every day, like what to eat, how much sleep to get, work/life balance affect you. Even making medical choices in an overwhelming system of Western medicine (1) and Alternative medicine (2), not only serve you now, but they serve you as you age, and when you are ready to pass.

Unfortunately, when it comes time to end our journey, something we will all experience, most of us have no idea how to listen to our bodies and allow the natural process of death to occur. Instead of allowing one of the most natural things to happen to you, you fear it and make choices to stay until you have your last breath, no matter the quality of life. That is why tapping into *The Body Within* now is so important. Tapping into *The Body Within* now while you are healthy allows for you to be connected later in life when you need it the most.

You are taught many things, from the time of birth on how to live, get a good job, plan for your future, and so forth. The one thing, as a society, you really don't talk about much or even teach about is how much power you have to heal yourself alongside the medicine you choose. By listening to your body, managing your health, and knowing that you can have control allows for you to create your own long healthy life along with your own peaceful death.

How do you manage your everyday health? How do you navigate an overwhelming medical system of Western and Alternative Medicine, combat chronic   pain,   and/or   illness,   age   gracefully,   and   die   a peaceful death? By getting to know YOU. Getting up close and personal with *The Body Within*.

It's that good angel/bad angel on your shoulder you see in cartoons except it's the true essence of who you are. *The Body Within* - good angel - argues with what I call our created (or misinterpreted) reality/bad angel. Your created reality is what you <u>believe</u> to be true, or what you <u>think</u> you want, or the beliefs that have been imposed upon you by society, family, or others in your life.

The Body Within is your good angel, and your mediator, to help you police yourself – to help you see what's actually happening around you, not what you interpret as happening and help you be the best you can be. It helps you know how to eat and sleep right, exercise, to reduce stress, and learn what makes you happy with family, careers, hobbies, friends, and so forth. The good angel is always alerting you if you need help in these areas. It's up to you to learn to listen.

The key to listening is to learn to balance yourself and your life around you so you can start intuitively hearing all the amazing messages just waiting for you.

What do I consider balance and why is it so important? Balance is the power of three: Body, Mind, and Spirit. I believe balancing all three can be difficult but worth it. And balance between Body, Mind, and Spirit must be equal! Yes, I did say <u>equal</u>! So, if all three are equal, that means you should pay attention to your Body, Mind, and Spirit every day! Yes, every day! This means you check in with all three every day or maybe thirty minutes before bed to make sure tomorrow is even better.

Your Body: How is your body doing? Does it need anything? Are you feeling tired? Maybe, some stretching? Was your nutrition sound today? Did you get any exercise today? Do you need exercise? Can you do better tomorrow?

Your Mind: Now you should think about your day. Check in to see if it was busy, manageable, and so forth. How did you handle issues that came your way? Did you see them clearly? Were you tired and unfocused? If you were unfocused, how was your nutrition? Were you sharp and on task?

Next, *The Body Within* (your good angel/bad angel), can you sense it at all? Was it alerting you to anything? Did you listen or did you overrule it? Just taking the time to self-evaluate daily connects and rebalances you and opens the door for change. My challenge to you, as I give you the tools is this: Try balancing all three and see the positive effect it has on you and your daily living. See if it helps you discover triggers for your chronic pain or health issues. See if it alters you to why your kids are misbehaving! See if it helps you view yourself in a clearer light to know if you are the reason why your boss is always on your case.

When you work to balance yourself, it creates quiet in your energy, this will help you to hear *The Body Within*. As you listen to *The Body Within*, life becomes less complicated, and the knowing inside teaches you how to live a truly fulfilling and productive life.

The most important part of connecting with *The Body Within* is it not only teaches you how to live, but it also teaches you that we are all here for a limited amount of time. This journey will end. The choices we make about how to live not only serve you now, but they serve you when you are ready to die. I know this sounds crazy – that you might have control over how you die, but I believe if you learn to listen now, you will automatically listen then.

Start reading, and I will share with you what I know. I'll show you that, if you balance your life and get to know *The Body Within*, the true essence of who you are, you can and will change your life for the here and now -- and the hereafter.

Happy reading! Marie
☺

The Come and Go

By McKayla Jordan

Everyone has to come, and we all have to go.
We come with a bang of joy and leave with a stream of tears.
We come and get showered with gifts. Then
leave and get covered with flowers.
Though it's easier to accept, then it is to give away.
In our hearts, our loved ones will stay.
And as we say goodbye we will rise to our Lord.
We will pray and thank him and smile for we have returned home.
Everyone has to come, and we all have to go...

CHAPTER 1

How the Body Heals In My Eyes

BEFORE I DESCRIBE HOW I interpret how the body heals I want to explain where I am generating this information from. I have combined my knowledge using all the tools I have acquired over the last 20 years of my healing work, my Exercise Science degree, my own personal journey of self-healing and body awareness. That does not mean this is exactly how the body heals—it is my interpretation. By using this knowledge, I have been able to help many people regain body health and wellness not thought possible in the scope of the Western and Alternative medical models along with helping them learn to use some of the skills in this book to help them self-heal themselves. My hope is it helps you too.

I see it as your feet are anchored to the ground. Your brain gives you the signal to move—your big toe pushes you off, your brain creates a series of events that propel you forward, and you walk. If the body is in sync with the nervous system, your body propels forward without costing you a lot of physical or emotional energy. When you are out of sync, it can cost you a lot of physical and emotional energy exhausting your body and weakening you physically over time. This is what is considered your economy of movement. Your feet are the foundation that keeps your whole body upright, healthy.

We are all born with an innate pattern to which the body knows what muscle fires at what time, so everything is in sequence - The nervous system oversees all of this. With all of this in sync, walking does not cost you energy.

When you walk, your hips swing in opposite direction of each other, which also swings your shoulders opposite of each other. Your arms swing without exerting effort, which then engages your core. This, in turn, alerts the core muscles to squeeze the middle of your torso, which not only holds you upright but as they are squeezing your midsection they are massaging your organs to detox your body, helping the body drain the lymph system and stimulating your digestion to process all the nutrients we consume in a day, as well as eliminate them. Some of this we know from science in connection with innate intelligence about your body you are born with.

My interpretation is whole health starts when all the movements are in sync, so movement does not cost you energy or block any systems from functioning fully. From the time we are in utero, to rolling down a hill for the first time, to walking, so much can happen to you such as sports injuries, illness, genetics, and so forth.,. However, once your economy of movement (or synchronicity) is compromised, your health starts to degrade. How does it become interrupted; you might ask?

My first answer to that is – Life.

When I work with my clients, I intuitively try to get them involved to help me "dissect," as I call it, their life.

After countless injuries, concussions, stress, physical and emotional trauma, surgeries, repetitive motion trauma, nutrition (or lack of proper nutrition), excessive workout or not working out, the body leaves a trail. The body has rewired the nervous system so many times it cannot find its way back home.

Let's say you are 18 months old, and your first injury is you fall off the couch and land hard on your side. You get up and cry, shake it off in a couple of days nobody remembers except your body. Now your pelvis is off to the right, which will throw your right foot off and your left shoulder. Now you do it again except you are 3, and you hit your head? Now your neck stiffens up, and you are already limited in your left shoulder so in order to heal it your body limits the movement in your right rib cage. Now you are six, and you're playing baseball, and you're just not as athletic as your parents would like. Your coordination is a bit off, but that's just you. Then you sprain your ankle fairly good on the right due to running. Now your gait is not as smooth as it should be, and your flexibility is limited due to the earlier issues.

Now your left hip must make up for all of that. Your body heals things up, but every time there is a new injury your fluid movement in your gait that moves your body forward, that never cost you any energy to walk before, now is costing you energy. It is also making a new pattern to do its best to keep you upright hence getting further and further from the innate knowledge your body was born with. Now maybe you are experiencing a headache or 2 a week but by the time you hit your teens and a couple more injuries you have fatigue, sometimes chronic migraines, headaches and just days where you don't feel energized. That's just who you are now.

Why do some people not react the same way to life and its accumulation? How we process stress weakens you. How you eat either can fuel you or weaken you. If your body is already struggling, you need to ramp up your nutrition and reduce stress to your body. If not, the body will weaken which just enhances the cycle. Even things like over worn or unstable shoes or an old couch or mattress can cost a person in chronic pain or illness their body's ability to expend energy toward their healing trying to stay balanced due to the body's just need to survive.

Now we go on into adulthood and I find by the time we hit mid-40s and especially 50s all of a sudden there has been so much life added on to your body with your nervous system changing each time working to find a new way to survive, the individual has no real understanding that things never healed completely and never regained full movement and flexibility. Now to walk across the floor, not only cost a lot of energy, but you now have to propel yourself across the floor versus your body being an object at rest staying at rest and an object in motion staying in motion with the same speed and in the same direction unless acted upon by an unbalanced force (Newton's First Law). This is outright exhausting.

I find most people with chronic pain, chronic illness, especially Lyme disease, are just that. Their body has endured so many reorganizations that they cannot walk across the room without it being a huge energy cost, not only physically but mentally as well. When you are in balance the body just moves, you exert no effort to create the outcome. When you are out of balance, the body must think more in order to move and then you have to push it forward. Now you're mentally exhausted just for being you. I call that the gift that just keeps on giving. So now the person's arms no longer swing, their abdominals no longer support their spine, and they have to contract any muscle available to hold them upright. Without their abdominals contracting as they walk their body does not massage the organs and intestines, there is no natural detox or elimination going on and they become stuck in a body that can't remember where home is.

I find the larger the injuries and stress to the body at a young age tend to leave a bigger imprint on how our body grows and moves over time. We assume these injuries heal and our body has corrected the movement, but instead what it has done is re-patterned around the injury to create a new gait pattern. This causes stress to our body over time, now adding repetitive motions, athletic injuries, car accidents, trips, falls, and so forth to the already challenged nervous system. From there it's hard to process any stress to the body. So, foods that are harder for the body to digest tax their intestines, so their body rejects them. Any air born chemicals, strong smells, or odors they come in contact with their body can't process because their toxic load is too high. It's too much work for the body to process these things, so the body will not allow them to enter. The body is smart. Its main goal is survival no matter how it affects you in the long run.

Physical activity of any kind is exhausting because to lift their leg the body now has to engage every other part of the body. I have seen migraine sufferers wiggle their toes and watch it pull on their jaw because their body is so out of sync. The body does not know it's supposed to fire the ankle, not the head to propel the body forward because the nervous system lost its connection a long time ago. The body is in what I call "survival mode."

Now your body is so tired just from everyday living it starts to become ill. There is no one thing that stands out that your doctor can test. You have all these sensitivities, allergies, asthma, fatigue, and so forth. If you choose to undergo extensive testing with Alternative practitioners, you find that your body is under severe stress. Then the practitioner starts medicines or supplements to try to either fix or band aid the problem, but what happens is your body can't process that either and it just confuses the body even more.

Your body has lost its innate ability to know how to heal, so it can't possibly process what it is being asked to do. The drugs give some relief, but after a while, the body becomes stressed by taking the medicines and then they don't have an affect anymore. Now you are out of sync and overwhelmed in a body that is just not serving you.

Energetically when I tap into *The Body Within* it tells me what the biggest drain on your body is at that moment and we work to correct it. That opens a window of opportunity for the body to lessen the load of stress and start to remember what it knew a long time ago. Each time I work with the individual, it happens the same way. Once we correct the stressor of that moment and reeducate the nervous system, I work with you to become more aware of your body. Your body heals a little bit more, gains a little more innate knowledge, and the cycle continues in a positive direction.

The healing is endless. I have seen young people, people in their 40s, 50s and now 70s and 80s regaining lost strength, mobility function and cognitive function. My hope is I can share this knowledge with you and help you facilitate your own healing. This not only serves the chronic pain population but anyone who wants to stay healthy and strong and out of nursing care as you age. We all have an accumulation of life which should impart wisdom to you. It should not cripple you and make you helpless as you age. The wisdom you have gained in life should empower you to be the best you that you can be at any age. That's what I call *The Body Within!*

The Body Within

CHAPTER 2

My Story

THIS PART OF MY STORY started around 1990 after my second child was born. She was born by C-section just like my first. There were some complications during delivery where I sustained an aggressive amount of bruising to my right side, and it took about six months to recoup, but it never seemed to feel the same after that. Shortly thereafter, I started to have a lot of right-sided pain in my shoulder and neck along with pain in my face. I had numbness and tingling down my hand constantly and was losing function in my arm. I was being treated for thoracic outlet syndrome. They said I had no space between my first rib and clavicle. As I started treatment, my daughter was almost ten months old. I thought things were challenging having two children and a lot of physical pain. Then, shortly after I find out I am five months pregnant. This was a surprise since I had had surgery after the last pregnancy to prevent it. I put on my big girl pants, started focusing on having a baby versus dealing with fighting with the pain in my arm and four months later I have three children.

I had him C-section as well, and the rehab went a lot better than with the second child, but the arm quickly became a real problem. Three little kids and an arm that did not want to cooperate and I was also going to school part-time to get my Exercise Science degree.

I started physical therapy, but it only seemed to make things worse. My doctor sent me to an orthopedic surgeon who said the only treatment they have right now was a radical surgery and it was experimental and did not generate good outcomes, suggesting that I should just live with it. I got another opinion that said the same thing. I was very frustrated and not sure what to do, but my personality has always been if you push hard enough, you will always get your answers.

My quest for answers brought me to a very well-known thoracic surgeon who worked in the same hospital as my mother-in-law and my husband. This surgeon gave me the answer I wanted to hear. He had done the surgery many times and always had good outcomes; it was a piece of cake for him.

To surgery, I went all along knowing what the other two doctors had said; I kept saying to myself "but everyone I know loves and trust this guy, they all look up to him as a 'god.'"

The surgery seemed to be a success. I woke up in the least amount of pain I had been in two years. No headache, no jaw pain, no arm pain. I was in heaven.

A noticeably short period of time went by, and something just did not feel right. I shared my concerns with the surgeon and all he kept saying was I was not trying hard enough to rehab it. Now anyone who knows me knows that is about as false of a statement you could ever make about me. Maybe overdoing it, but under-doing? Nope!

Every day got harder and harder, and now my scapula (wing bone) in my back was sticking out so I could not sit back in a chair. The more I complained, my world seemed to turn against me. The surgeon was counseling my closest family members on my lack of progress. He said it was my fault and their narrow vision that a doctor is always right stopped them from seeing the pain I was really in.

I was alone in my world, and I was the only one that feels this is a problem.

I went to my primary doctor who finally believed me and sent me to a Doctor of Physical Therapy to get his opinion. He felt I might have suffered long thoracic nerve injury during surgery and sent me to a neurologist right away.

I was getting ready for my appointment when the phone rang. It was the surgeon. He said he was sent a copy of the report and wanted to know my symptoms and what the Doctor of Physical Therapy thought. I told him the same as I told him many times before about my physical issues and that the Doctor of physical therapy thought it was long thoracic nerve injury. The phone got quiet. He then said "I could have cut the nerve; I am not sure. Let me know how it turns out." Then abruptly hung up the phone. What could I say?

I had my nerve tests done, and it was determined it was nerve damage, could take three or so years to correct itself, if at all. So, I would need a lot of physical therapy.

My already solo journey just got lonelier. I not only find out the devastating news that my right side is really messed up but instead of the family support I had hoped for, I now became the elephant in the room. Nobody asked about me; I was not allowed to talk about it. The attitude was because this doctor was God, everyone knew him and saw him on a regular basis, and they wanted me to pretend it never happened. Nobody even talked about it—he wronged me, but it was a forbidden topic. It was a trying time for me, as parents from both sides needed surgery for health reasons, and I would steer them away from the same doctor, but because he didn't make a mistake with me, it's ok to use him. The outcomes were not good, but somehow those all had reasons other than it could be his skills. It was like I was living in a completely different world than everyone else around me. He still does surgery today, and now I get his patients who are trying to recover from not so positive outcomes. I call it the gift that keeps on giving.

I was set up for physical therapy and was informed that I was one of 20 cases documented, so there is no real treatment, there is only 'figuring it out as we go.' I could no longer support my shoulder and arm myself, so the physical therapist put me in a brace to hold it up. Unfortunately, the brace was not a good fit for my problem, and it caused a lot of damage to the surrounding muscles and caused my right leg to be more involved. So, my entire right side was not working properly.

At this point, my insurance was an HMO new to our area, and I was informed that my 20 visits were up, and I would have to pay out of pocket. This was not an option. I appealed to my insurance even though the physical therapist told me "no one ever gets extensions, don't even try." Well, I was approved for endless visits, and I was so happy. Then two visits later, the physical therapist told me I was getting so much better that he was releasing me, and I did not need any more care. He wrote in my report that I was almost healed.

I panicked and went back to the neurologist. And he said all his reports say things are so much better, so I have no way to know different. He said he has been working with the physical therapist for years and he is never wrong. All along I kept saying, but I am not better. I was beginning to think I was crazy.

As I researched and looked for answers, I found that the physical therapist got paid the same amount for treating me once as he did 40 times from the HMO. That explained a lot, except for what I was supposed to do.

Five months into it, I was on my own as a part-time student, a full- time mom of three little ones, and a full-time rehab person for myself. This personal rehab consisted of a very strong healing diet, focus on my physical body as well as rest and any nutritional supplement that boosted my immune system. School was hard because writing and typing were very difficult, but I figured out ways of recording classes and begging for help from friends and teachers. The best part was my major being Exercise Science because was able to pick the brains of the professors and did my internships with people I knew could help. I knew I needed to keep learning about muscles and their movements, so I was not giving up.

Money was nonexistent at this point, so I decided to go for Social Security disability to help me while I try to figure this out. I met with four different lawyers who proceeded to tell me one after the other that I did not look like the person depicted in my medical records, that I need to stop trying to fix things and let nature take its course. Get on some medications, gain some weight, and look more disabled. I was shocked. I was not able to sit or stand for any length of time, no lifting, cooking, I could not even fold laundry. I spent most of my awake hours on the floor on my back with my kids playing around me. And I am told I have to look like this is real. I wasn't sure what that meant but I was shaken.

Then I was referred to a different lawyer who said this is crazy; your records are your records; I will take your case and we will work on pursuing the doctor after. Off to court we went, and the judge threw it out stating I was not the person depicted in these records. Called me a liar. I was stunned. We appealed, and he threw this out as well. My lawyer said he was sorry, but I am not going to win even with the doctor, so he wished me well and gave me back my files.

At this point, it was the first time I truly hit rock bottom. I went home and cried to my husband, but instead of consoling me he said maybe it's not as bad as I think it is. He suggested maybe going back to work to see what happens, that we could really use the money. I could not believe what he was saying!

Well, I guess there was a bigger bottom than I thought. I did not know where they were coming from but suddenly, I just started shouting, "I'm going to fix myself, and I will help others too!"

He looked at me and said, "If this is the way it's going to be, you have to accept it so you can move on." I shouted it again and again and by the third time I knew it was true. I did not know how, but I knew it was true. There was nothing left to be said and only one direction to go in.

A short period of time went by with few words from me around my family and friends; I was still the elephant in the room but an even bigger one. The doctor said I was not trying hard enough; the physical therapist said I was fine. The lawyers said I was not the person in my records, and I had been told by a judge to get over myself. I must really be crazy.

I was now picking the brains of every professor in school and really focusing on my body from the inside out to cooperate. If there was a way to fix things, I was going to find it. Then someone slipped me the name of a new doctor in the area who works from a more untraditional view. His name was Dr. SU. He took one look at me and my crooked malfunctioning body and said, "I only know one physical therapist (Linda) in the area that might be able to help. She does integrative therapy," (a very specialized form of physical therapy) "and may be able to point you in a more positive direction."

I went to Linda and she told me that she learned in a clinic in Connecticut. She maps the body with energy medicine and uses trained techniques to help release scar tissue and realign muscles and tissue to bring back healthy blood flow to those areas. After doing her assessment, she said I could work with her every day for ten years and barely make a dent. She knew I was in school for Exercise Science, so she asked me to learn some releases on myself to make faster progress. I was all in. She would show me something, and I would go home and try it, but then I would see a different more productive way to do it for my body. I never gave it much thought that I should not know a different way, I just kept learning. She would smile when I showed her and then she would show me something else.

Once again, my insurance ran out, but this time I was not distressed. I now had so many tools. I just kept my focus; I had been down this road before, but this time was very different. I was not looking for answers, I was my answer.

Her parting words to me were, "Start studying energy medicine and you will be teaching me in a few years." I laughed and went on my way.

The more I worked on myself, the more I started to see pictures in my mind of the bones, muscles, and tissue and where they were restricted. It made me aware of how to correct things, but it also made me aware of all the surgeries and injuries to my body all had to be reversed in order for me to regain my health back.

Then one day my daughter came home from soccer with an injured knee. I knew right away it was a sprain, but then I felt at that moment I should try to do to her what I had been doing on myself. I laid my hands on her knee, I saw the twist between the knee and ankle, was able to help her realign the leg, and she walked away so much better.

Now that screaming moment with my husband started flooding back. I was going to help myself and help others too. Yup, it all started to make sense.

The more I shared with friends, the more people let me try on them. As time went on, word got out to a woman who owned an office with holistic practitioners and she offered me space, to do what I do. I laughed and said I don't even know what I do. She that's ok, people will come. She offered to get me started by supplying me, clients. Now here I am, 18 years later, still learning and seeing more new ways the body heals every day and helping countless amounts of people learn about themselves and become their own answer.

CHAPTER 3

The Awakening

FOUR OF US SIT in my mother-in-law's hospital room: There is me, my husband, and her two daughters. She has an older son, Joe, but no one is aware he is missing currently. Though Grace is in the final days of cancer, she looks peaceful and her small hands rested on the white blanket. I wonder, does she know she's dying? Sadness hangs in the air, but there is also a sense of relief that she's not going to suffer anymore.

Once cancer reached a critical point in her body before the pain became commonplace, Grace just seemed to make a decision. She was ready to go. It was extremely quick. For all of us, these were some of the most challenging days of our lives. Why did it happen so fast? It seems as if she knew her fight was over, but we thought we would have more time. She didn't really seem all that sick.

Suddenly, everything just came to a head. Now, here we are at the hospital. There are so many people – friends, extended family, and closest family, all here to comfort a woman who always comforted them. Suddenly, we're alerted that she's starting to die. Friends quickly exit the room. Her children and I rush in. It was just like in the movies. A couple of deep breaths and she was gone. It was beautiful!

The energy in the room stills, while the quiet sobs of Grace's two daughters create an ominous echo. My husband, Grace's younger son, and I stand by, hugging one another. I could feel him mourning but in a more private way. I moved away from him to let my own feelings come to the surface. I am momentarily distracted as I realize her oldest son is not here. My heart sinks for Joe, the older son, knowing that he missed his final moment with the one person he loved and trusted most in life. How was he going to handle not saying goodbye? Less than a minute or two later, a relative who was outside the room, says, "Joe is on his way. He was in the lobby getting on the elevator." Now, everyone in the room realizes Joe is missing, and there is panic on their faces.

As I stand there, I start to feel the energy in the room change from very somber to a state in which I feel a strong, energetic pull in my direction, which startles me. Then, a strange awareness comes over me. At that moment, I realize that Grace knows that Joe is not in the room.

Grace was not only my mother-in-law, but she also supported me from the first when I became a Healing Arts Practitioner. She admitted that she did not understand what it was, or how it worked, but she knew, deep down that I was different, and this is what I should be doing.

As I settled into the energy shift in the room, I knew what I needed to do. My mind is in a state of 'I know what I need to do but can she really do what she wants to do?' I slowly walked away from the bed. All eyes were on Grace as she lay lifeless in her just-passed energy. As I moved to the corner of the room, I raised my hands and simply gave energy to the scenario unfolding in front of me. My intuition told me what was going to happen, but my brain said, you are nuts! This can't happen." I just kept getting the feeling that all I needed to do was hold space and be open; the rest will take care of itself.

About a minute, maybe two passed; it seemed like hours. Then it happened. Grace started to breathe again. It was a little scary at first, but then she started to breathe in a rhythm as if she's coming back to life. All eyes were fixed on Grace, wondering why this is happening.

The door opens. Joe ran in, grabbed his mother's hand, and told her, "I'm here." As he held her hand, her breathing became normal. Joe said to her, "Mom, I love you. It's okay to go," and again, just like in the movies, a few short breaths, an exhale, and she was gone. Joe's rugged frame sagged, and he moved away from the bed.

I was still standing in the corner holding space, watching as if I were at a performance. The mood around the bed was solemn. I'm stunned, excited, happy, but also deeply saddened that she was actually gone. I started coming back to reality and tried to process what had just happened. How did she do that? Can we all do this? Why did Grace do this for her son? The answers came in a flood of awareness, experiences I have had with this family over the past 25 years. Grace knew that after Joe's dad died, Joe's life was very challenging for years. She knew, of all her children, Joe was the one who needed to say goodbye, or he would struggle for a long time. It was her last act as a loving, devoted, matriarch of her family.

As I stood by in dismay, not having the slightest idea how to process any of it, I became aware of all the different interactions in the room. Grace is gone, her children are consoling each other while I'm in the same room, but on the outside looking in. I have so much on my mind. Her loss seems so minimal knowing that she is ok and still in control on the other side.

As we all pitched in to pack up Grace's belongings before heading home, the children were focused on her dying and how life is going to be without her. Nothing was said, there is no discussion. At that point, I'm not sure myself what happened. For the next few days, I think about what I had witnessed, still shocked, while trying to support everyone from the monumental loss we had all suffered. I knew, in time, it would all sort itself out.

The Body Within

CHAPTER 4

It Is What It Is

SO WHY GRACE? Why was she able to control her ending so beautifully?

Grace was one of the most realistic people I have ever met. She was a little too worrisome in life, which made it hard for people to see her in her true glory. She was an observer of life, and her life's choices brought her to her defining moment in her hospital room with her children. For 15 years, Grace worked in housekeeping on the oncology floor of a hospital.

She not only cleaned patient rooms, but she talked with them, the nurses, and the doctors. She observed life at its most vulnerable and she saw some of the good, and some of the most painful moments, for many. Grace cared for a lot of patients, and their families, and comforted them in their struggles. She always knew, someday, it might be her own or a family member that might need the wisdom that she had accumulated over time. She also knew that all her observations and life experiences were going to guide her eventually.

Before Grace was diagnosed with cancer, she had been complaining for a long time of cramping and bloating in her abdominal area. Her doctor at the time was not listening to her concerns, so she changed doctors. Immediately they did an ultrasound and determined she needed a hysterectomy.

Unfortunately, when they performed the surgery, they found that cancer had been there too long, and there was nothing more they could do. They did not offer her treatments, give her any options or hope.

This was unacceptable to Grace. She felt her time was limited, but she did not feel that the time was now. She felt deep down there was more she could do. She armed herself with information and sought the help of a family member in the medical field. She told the doctors, "This is what I want for treatment and you have to try at least." Grace could be forceful when she wanted to be.

The doctors conceded and into remission Grace went. For about five years, Grace was enjoying the extra time she had, but rest assured she had no blinders on that she still had to be aware of her body and what was happening. Then, the cancer returned. Doctors told her she had to go on chemo indefinitely this time. Grace told them she would decide when and for how long she would use chemo. Grace did the treatments as recommended. I remember sitting there with her when she said, "It's enough." My heart pounded, as I said, "What do you mean?" She responded, "I feel good, and I know if I continue the treatments, they will make me sick, not the cancer. So, I'm done with treatments." The doctors did not agree. They said if she stopped it would come right back. She disagreed. Three years passed.

She was working in my office one day and came to my door to talk to me. She looked at me, and at that moment, I knew. I said, "It's back, again isn't it?" She said, "Yes. They haven't told me yet, but I know." The desk I stood behind seemed to grow and I felt like it was creating a distance between us. It was like I was protecting myself because my gut was telling me she was not going to fight any more. I asked her what she was thinking, and she said, "I'm ok, I miss my husband. You kids are grown, I'm ok!" I knew at that moment Grace had made a decision. Now I just had to support her vision. This time, she took a different approach. She took a step back and let the doctors choose everything. Never asked questions, did not research anything, just went along with what she was told, not what she believed was right for her. She went through treatments to help her kids heal. She went from being in charge to giving up her power. Little did I realize, she kept it the whole time.

Grace had her own vision of how she wanted life to be. She knew if she got sick and it was terminal, it didn't have to be painful. She knew death shouldn't be feared; it's part of life. We are all here for a certain amount of time, and in her wisdom, she understood that sometimes it's not about quantity, it's about quality. Grace knew her truth and knew the direction her life was headed. She may have appeared weak to those around her, but under it all, she was an extraordinarily strong woman.

You see, twelve years before, her husband John died of colon cancer. In the end stages of his cancer, John's kidneys started to fail, and his doctors wanted to put a stent, a small mesh tube, in to help drain them. Grace didn't want that because she knew, from all she had seen, that if he died from kidney failure, he would get a high fever, go into a coma, and die peacefully. Inserting a stent meant, yes, he would have more time with his family, and yes, she would cherish it dearly, but she knew John would probably die from cancer, not kidney failure, and his death would be more drawn out and painful. She felt sometimes nature had a way of handling things and we should respect and appreciate its wisdom.

John and his doctors really felt more time was the better option, so they decided on putting in the stent. Grace was disappointed he made that decision. She was happy for the extra time but wished that things could have been handled more naturally and kindly. From early on, Grace knew her truth about life and death.

After John had chosen his treatment, it was only a short time later that his ending was as she expected, not only for him but for his family. When cancer than infected Grace and it was getting closer to her time, Grace took the opposite approach and wouldn't allow her doctors to do anything that would prolong her life. She valued quality not quantity.

Grace knew, at an intuitive level inside herself, that death is as beautiful as birth. If we can understand that and fear it less, it can be an amazing exchange of wisdom and love for everyone involved.

I am telling you this story because we have experiences every day that we give no time or attention to. They are our answers to living a more present and directed life. *The Body Within* was written to help you become more aware of your surroundings and all the messages that fuel the direction of the choices you make toward healing illness, getting the perfect job, raising a family, caring for loved ones or just living a positive peaceful existence.

Your intuition, your life awareness, and your choices made from them is knowing *The Body Within*.

Grace tapped into her intuition, her Body Within (though she didn't really call it that or anything) throughout her journey and it gave her power and clarity in making choices that gained her more time with her family. My guess is she always had intuition but did not feel comfortable showing it until the first doctor ignored her and realized her not speaking up had cost her so much already. That cost her time and quality of life with her family. Unfortunately, that is how most of us wake up. I personally would like to see you awake without having to hit a wall of adversity in order to see the true healer you have inside. My goal in this book is to help you know that part of you long before you are faced with a life or death situation. Knowing it now not only serves you now but, like Grace, also when you pass.

Grace was an amazing teacher. I would like to take a moment and end this chapter with a toast to my mother-in-law, my friend, and my teacher. Thank you, Grace.

CHAPTER 5

Mary

MARY IS A 13-YEAR-OLD girl I met some time ago. She was very shy, beautiful with dark hair and struggled with her weight. Her mom, Suzanne, had taken Mary to the doctor for abdominal pain on her right side. The doctor thought her appendix was the problem, so he performed surgery. Unfortunately, it was an incorrect diagnosis. While in surgery, the doctor explored her abdominal cavity, but he didn't find anything to explain her symptoms. Next, he ordered a lot of tests like an upper GI, lower GI, colonoscopy, barium enema, and so forth. They still couldn't find the cause of Mary's pain. Bed rest was the only thing that seemed to help but was also complicating things. After three months of bed rest, multiple diagnostic tests, and homeschooling, Suzanne and Mary still didn't have answers. The treatment plan was to start Mary on pain management at the pain center or go in surgically again to look around. Suzanne and Mary had already made a few trips to a large hospital in Boston.

Suzanne had been referred to me through some of her friends; I met her and Mary at their home. I told them I would do my best to help. I took a complete history of previous injuries. Mary fell and split her head open four years prior, broke her fifth rib two years prior on the right side, and twisted her right knee six months before pain onset. I watched Mary in her bed, curled up like a ball, and as soon as she straightened her body, the pain flared up. If she laid still, there was no pain, it was all movement activated.

As I tapped into Mary's energy, I could sense the pain was coming from what some practitioners call myofascial pain syndrome. Myofascial pain is caused by the misalignment of fascia surrounding the muscles. This can be caused by injury, surgery, or weak musculature. When muscles atrophy from lack of use, the tissue around the muscle shrinks and twists. Getting up and moving the area (exercise) helps increase the blood flow to the muscles and strengthens them to pull the fascia straight. Sometimes it works itself out easily, but in Mary's case, her sedentary lifestyle, the extra injuries, and now surgical scar tissue made the already adhered fascia twist and adhere to different parts of the body.

When muscles sustain an injury to their fibers, the surrounding fascia shortens and tightens in response to the injury. Unequal muscle tension can cause compression of both nerves and muscles, resulting in pain. In a lot of ways, it's considered phantom pain. Thankfully, there is a lot of research currently being done to scientifically prove how fascia affects the body from a rehabilitation standpoint. In British Columbia, the Fascia Research Congress held a conference as a collaboration of clinicians and scientists sharing and learning to progress the field of fascia research. (To find out more go to FasciaCongress.org.) There are a lot of physical therapists, massage therapists, and personal trainers also working with these theories as well.

If we look at Mary's past injuries, they were all to the right side of her body. Her lifestyle was sedentary, and she was housebound and overweight. Physically, her muscles were weak, to begin with, and there was no stability in her core to hold her spine upright. This caused the muscles to weaken and the fascia and scar tissue to twist. A strong core and spine keep you upright and erect, whereas a weak one will not allow that. A lot of times you are weak before you get injured. Then after the injury, it becomes so much harder to heal and exercise, so without a strong core, you become weaker. It's a destructive cycle and a main cause of chronic pain. Look around at society –

your peers, coworkers, family – and you'll see how sedentary lifestyles and work environments contribute to the problem. Especially troubling are the children who spend countless hours on computers and video games instead of engaging in physical activity such as sports and outdoor play. This does not bode well for their future health.

After energetically assessing Mary, I was able to pinpoint exactly what I felt was going on. From there, I did my good practitioner duty. I said to Suzanne, "There's a good chance this is myofascial pain syndrome. I know a physical therapist with excellent credentials and experience in this area. You should take Mary to see her for an evaluation." The reason I did not do an energetic release at that time is Suzanne had health insurance and I am a 'self-pay'. I felt they could get their answers from medicine as finances were an issue, so I always explore that avenue first. Suzanne was excited that there might be an answer, after all. Suzanne talked to the doctors and gave them all the information. They refused to send Mary to a physical therapist. They said the information I provided wasn't an adequate diagnosis, and that Suzanne should proceed with the specialist's recommendations. Suzanne tried to present her case again, but there was no support.

Suzanne decided to bring Mary to my office to see if I could help. In one visit, Mary was walking upright. In four visits, she was pain-free. Then, the hard part began. Because Mary was in bed for three months, her weak muscle tone, bone loss, and weight gain made her a must for physical therapy, but the doctors wouldn't send her to a physical therapist. They felt the problem was resolved without Western medical intervention, so Mary must have been faking. Suzanne and her daughter would have to do this on their own. At that point, they were overwhelmed and bewildered. Neither one has ever exercised or had a real understanding of what they were being asked to do. As much as I explained why the energy treatment helped, Suzanne and Mary, didn't completely understand. They tried to educate themselves about weak muscle tone and why the risk of re-injury was so high. Lack of knowledge and support from a familiar place – their doctors – made the situation even more difficult. It was definitely myofascial twisting. However, the condition was so foreign to the doctors and mother and daughter and using energy to help resolve it just didn't make sense. They only cared that the pain was gone, and now Mary could get back to her life. As weak as she was and lying down for much of the previous three months, Mary was prone to continue myofascial twisting and injury.

In other words, without strengthening, Mary was an accident waiting to happen. I did the best I could. I provided information, but the rest was up to them. We had our ups and downs, but eventually, Mary was doing very well. I had not seen them for six months when Suzanne brought Mary back to see me. According to Suzanne, Mary has had a severe headache since her tonsils were removed a month ago. Considering her history, I strongly suspected that the tissue and fascia around Mary's cervical vertebrae and shoulders became twisted during the recovery period following the surgery. I suggested to Suzanne that she should get a referral to a chiropractor or an osteopath. Either would be a perfect match. Just like MD's, an Osteopath (Doctor of Osteopathic Medicine) completes four years of medical school and can practice in any specialty. In addition, they receive 300-500 hours in the study of osteopathic manipulative treatment and the body's musculoskeletal system. I gave Suzanne names for both so she would have more information to bring to her doctor. Surely, this was something Mary's doctors would be very familiar with and should be able to help.

Unfortunately, once again there was no support for Mary and her mom. The recommendations were not within the scope of what Western medicine would consider a proven treatment. So, what was Mary's mom to do? Suzanne had changed their primary care at this point, and the same outcome prevailed. Once again, Suzanne was at a complete loss and needing a referral from her insurance, so her hands were tied. She brought Mary back to see me, to work with the energy treatment, and in one visit the pain was less than half. A few more visits and Mary was pain-free--for now. Once again, I counseled them on myofascial twisting and stressed the need for Mary to lose weight and strengthen, or she was prone to future injuries.

Mary did well for a year and a half, and then she and Suzanne were back on my doorstep. This time, it was a severe migraine that had been going on for three weeks. She was on the latest and greatest of pain medications with no relief. Mary was now fifteen. I had taken another lifestyle history, and two weeks before the headaches started, Mary started kickboxing classes. Mind you, she was not continually active before this. Is the bell going off in your head too? Weak body. Aggressive exercise. I energetically scanned Mary's back, neck, and shoulder area and I could sense the muscles were very tight and spasmed. When your muscles are strained and overworked, they create inflammation. This creates tightness in the muscles, nerves, and surrounding tissue areas. Could this be the cause of a longstanding headache?

I asked Suzanne if the doctors checked the muscles in Mary's neck and shoulders. "No," she said. "The doctor said it was migraines, so it's neurological." Then I asked Mary if she knew her neck and shoulders were that tight, and she replied, "Yes." So, I asked Mary why she didn't tell the doctor, and she responded, "They said it was migraines, so it didn't matter." In Suzanne and Mary's mind, migraines have no relation to her exercise. Would it have made a difference to the doctor? To some, it should, but we will never know. If you study anatomy, you know that the nerves run along, or in, the muscles. If the muscles are tight, the nerves must also be. There are different types of migraines, but this was muscular.

We addressed the problem with the same course of energy treatment, and Mary's headaches improved with one to two more energy sessions. Again, I counseled them on stretching and strengthening, suggested yoga or Pilates and walking until Mary was stronger.

Now, let's look at Mary's situation more closely. Is there a right or wrong party? Well, it must be the doctors, right? Or, wrong? You tell me. All the doctors treated Mary with the information available to them. The primary care doctor was at a loss, so he sent her to a surgeon. The surgeon found nothing, so he referred her to a gastroenterologist. He found nothing, based on his area of knowledge, so he sent her to a neurologist. The neurologist could not find anything, so that must be it. Mary was not experiencing pain in her knee, foot, hip, rib or anywhere that would cause her to be sent to an orthopedist. Even then, would he have found anything to explain her pain?

Myofascial pain syndrome is relatively new to Western medicine, but some physical therapists, massage therapists, and osteopaths are trained to work with it to help manage pain. It is a real medical condition, and when these practitioners encounter patients who have it, they're able to achieve good results. I have found through all the people I have seen over the years, being diagnosed with chronic pain, chronic illness, some auto-immune illness and even some Lyme Disease is just that, myofascial pain syndrome. The body has sustained so many reorganizations, as I call it, from injuries, illness, repetitive motion, childbirth, etc. The body becomes twisted, as I see it, then it has trouble detoxing itself due to the lack of proper gait, scar tissue, along with all kinds of physical stress and emotional stress. Then on top of everything else that the body is so out of balance it just does not remember the innate ability it was born with to heal itself. This was Mary's problem.

The doctor exhausted all his resources, but then Suzanne came to him with new information to consider. Shouldn't he have acted on it, or at least explored a little further? Each time Suzanne went back to the doctor, he should not have dismissed the information just because he did not believe it. If the doctor had taken the time to do a little research, he would have discovered that myofascial pain was a possibility, and there are other modalities in Western medicine like physical therapy he could have used. Why didn't he?

What about Suzanne? What is her role in this medical maze? Perhaps she should have changed primary care doctors again and again until she found one who was willing to listen. Is insurance set up for us to do that? She tried once and failed. What's the cost to continue to change doctors and what are the insurance hassles? At what point do you start to feel the doctor must be right and you must be wrong, especially when there is no validation for what your gut is telling you? Knowing what happened the first time with the belly pain, didn't that give Suzanne more information to handle the second and third times?

Should Suzanne have done some reading to learn how to prevent her daughter from being in this situation over and over? Or maybe Suzanne should have helped Mary understand that her lifestyle needed to change? Help her realize that she needed better nutrition and exercise after being sick so many times for so long? Shouldn't this have been Suzanne's priority? Then again, how was Suzanne to know it should be her priority if the doctors said it had nothing to do with Mary's illnesses? Finally, if Suzanne convinced Mary to change her lifestyle, would Suzanne have had to change hers as well?

What about Mary? She told me that she thought her headaches might be coming from that area, but since the doctor was so confident it was migraines, she did not mention it. Why didn't Mary think her opinion mattered? Should someone have taught her that her opinion mattered?

How could things have gone differently for Mary and Suzanne? What I can say is that everyone involved -- the doctors, Suzanne, and Mary – used the information they had available until more possibilities came their way. However, once there were more avenues to explore, why did all three of them shut them down?

As a society, we live in reaction mode. Your beliefs, fears, current knowledge, and desires come first before logic ever sees the light of day. This is where learning about *The Body Within* is crucial to short term and long-term health and wellness. When someone tries to tell you something, does reaction mode activate and prevent you from processing new information? We all do it. When Suzanne gave the doctor information that was unfamiliar to him, he drew back to his roots and shut down. That's reaction. Had he listened and been a bit curious, he may have seen the bigger picture. Suzanne and Mary did the same thing with the doctors. The doctor said "No," so instead of insisting that he looks further, or even insisting on the referral, Suzanne reacted and retreated. It never occurred to her to challenge the doctor because that's not what she was taught.

If Suzanne and the doctor were not in reaction mode, each could have heard what the other said and maybe, just maybe, a different outcome would have unfolded. The doctors tapped all their resources, but then new information came their way. What happened? That's when what the practitioners believe comes forward. Once they go through the available science and treatments, you will get what the practitioner believes. Then, you need to look at your healthcare provider. What do you really know about what they think of Alternative or Western medicine? Do they practice what they preach? Eat right, exercise and get enough rest? Do they think it matters? Do you? Remember, when doctors, naturopaths, nurse practitioners, acupuncturists, and so forth, exhaust their usual medical protocols, are they willing to see more options? Just remember to ask yourself, how well do I know them?

I'm fortunate to live close to Dartmouth-Hitchcock Medical Center. It is a Western medical and teaching facility with some of the best doctors and scientific research in the country. Every year, the hospital presents a community lecture series to teach the public about health. In 2001, the lecture series was called "Heal Thyself." It was an eight-week series, and each week a topic was devoted to how patients can help themselves, in partnership with their doctor.

I'll never forget it. They put up a map of the United States, and it was labeled "lumpectomy versus mastectomy." This was in reference to breast cancer treatments and how they compare across the country. The first slide illustrated that the science proved, in most cases, a lumpectomy was as equally effective as a mastectomy surgery. After showing the science, they put up the percentage of surgeons who performed a lumpectomy instead of a mastectomy. It was only about 25 percent. This meant that women unnecessarily received full mastectomies when a lumpectomy would have been equally effective. The medical faculty presenters asked the audience if anyone knew why. This was the shocker. Even though the science proved that the lumpectomy was equally effective in most cases, the surgeon felt that the mastectomy was better. Their point was, "Do your homework!" Doctors read the science but, in the end, you'll get what they think and feel, not necessarily the facts.

The presenters of this particular lecture couldn't stress enough how important it is that a patient knows the science too, and then make a decision based on what you feel is right for you. Sometimes, you'll think the same as the doctor. Other times, you'll disagree and do more research. But if you don't take the time to educate yourself, and just do what you're told, it may cost you an unnecessary surgery or treatments that could totally change your quality of life, or even end your life. It's your body; it's your choice. Make the choice because you know it's the right one for you, not because the doctor said so.

I want to help you develop and foster your intuition, what I consider *The Body Within*, so you will have keen awareness when dealing with chronic pain illness or even just wanting the best information for whole health and healthy aging. I want you to be able to embrace new information, process it, and make a choice whether it's right for you –or not. Learning this now will make you stronger and more directed in your health choices. This not only serves you now, but it will serve you later as well.

Keep reading and process the questions of the next few chapters. In Chapter 6, I will give you energy tools to help you wake up *The Body Within* and you will see how using it daily will help make better, healthier choices. You will learn to live a balanced, fulfilled life and be open to creating a balanced, peaceful ending when it is time.

The Body Within

CHAPTER 6

Sam

SAM WAS A 40-YEAR-OLD MALE diagnosed with terminal liver cancer. He was tall with grayish brown hair, very thin from the cancer and had lost the beautiful smile you could see hidden beneath the pain he was in. His furnishings were simple and represented his quiet, thoughtful nature. I met him during the end stage of his illness and offered my services as an energy practitioner to help him with his passing. I visited him at his home where he was bedridden, unable to eat, and severely jaundiced. I worked with his energy above his body and followed the guidance I was given. As I did this, I felt the direction very strongly and followed my intuition to clear his energy and work to create healing. It seemed like he was directing energy flow to his liver and creating health instead of working to pass on. I was puzzled. This is not what normally happens when someone is in this situation.

The next day, Sam called to tell me that he felt a lot better and was able to eat. He asked if I could come again. We did this a couple more times and then he asked if we could meet at my office. Every time I had worked with Sam, I went to his home where he was in bed, so I didn't know if he could make it up my office stairs. To my pleasant surprise, I opened my office door – at that time I was the second floor with no elevator - and there stood Sam with a big smile on his face.

Remarkably, he made the trip himself and said he felt good. We continued our sessions and focused on the fact that his healing was coming from within. Sam was healing himself. We also talked about the importance of proper nutrition and rest, and how this would help prolong his time with his family.

Sam and I had worked together for about two months, and things were going well. One day, he came in for his treatment, and his energy had taken a turn. He was no longer clearing his core flow, what I consider creating overall balance and health. Instead, he was taking healing energy into the belly area, mostly in the intestines. My first thought was that cancer had progressed, and Sam had taken our sessions as far as he could. I asked him about this because it was such a dramatic difference since our last session. Sam admitted that he had started on a cancer detox program he read about online. The program was based on a popular book, and the website touted many testimonials, so it was considered reputable.

Sam explained, "I was assigned a case worker that would help me with my treatments. This person is walking me through the protocol of drinking tinctures and then chasing them down with juice. This was quickly followed up with enemas to get the tincture out of his system because, apparently, it was somewhat toxic." Although it was toxic, it was supposed to rid his body of his cancer. I didn't know what to say. I wondered, does this even work? What is the evidence that it works other than a website with testimonials? Who are these people coaching Sam? If he found it online, how many other people are using this and who is documenting the validity of it if you do it at home? The caseworker told Sam he had been given a death sentence with his cancer diagnosis and this was his only hope to survive. They convinced Sam that this cancer detox program had worked many times and they called him to offer comfort and encouragement during the detox process.

Shocking? Not really. You see, when Sam was diagnosed as terminally ill, he talked with his doctors about Alternative options. They discouraged him, and he said it made him feel lost and scared. Sam considered our healing work together to be Alternative medicine (not a complement to medicine, which is what I consider myself) and since our sessions were giving him more time, Sam concluded that all Alternative medicine must work. Hence, he refused to stop the detox program. I emphasized to Sam that I was complementary to medicine, a healing facilitator, and not all Alternative medicines are reputable. Ultimately, I told Sam, "You are healing yourself." But Sam wouldn't, or couldn't, believe that. In my experience, this is the hardest concept for people to wrap their heads around -- that you really <u>can</u> heal yourself. Why do you feel you don't have the power to heal yourself? Don't forget to ponder that question <u>now</u> and at the end of the chapter.

As we continued our energy treatments, Sam would intermittently stop the detox program and begin to heal. However, it wasn't long before the caseworker would persuade him to start up again. Once again, his energy would drop. It was a roller coaster ride watching Sam try to grasp the reality that he could be the one keeping his body going. He just couldn't trust that it was all him, so he continued to try more alternatives. He started using them simultaneously, with no real understanding of what they were or their effect on his body. He was living in reaction to his fear of death and, in turn, not making decisions that were beneficial to him.

Meanwhile, I watched Sam's personal battle with himself, and how his energy changed according to where his head was. One day, he was in control of his healing and his core flow was strong and focused. The next day, he was confused and giving in to everyone else. That's when his energy became weak and scattered. What's worse is Sam was in a lot of pain and the people from the detox program discouraged him from taking morphine because, in their words, "Once you are on morphine, you are done." Instead, they told him to take cayenne pepper drinks.

Sam's distraught wife watched in horror as he struggled with his own mortality. All she wanted was for Sam to be at peace and enjoy his remaining time with her and their children. Unfortunately, Sam was unable to come to peace with himself, and he pushed his family away. In the end, his death was lonely and painful.

Is this a rare occurrence? I'm saddened to say it's not. I have had many similar experiences in my work, and they are becoming more common. Why does this happen? Can you do anything to stop it from happening to someone else? I believe that you really need to learn about who you are and what role you play in your own healing in order to avoid these circumstances. My way is to connect to *The Body Within*. My goal is to help you connect long before you become sick, so you will be more confident in making choices and Sam's story does not become a reality for someone else.

Let's pick apart Sam's story a bit:

Sam's doctors did everything humanly possible, within their scope of knowledge, to help him. But when Sam asked his doctors about Alternative options, Sam said they discouraged him from using any modalities. They did not offer Sam any guidance. Healing goes beyond what science has to offer. Doctors forget that desperate people do desperate things. Sam's doctors saw him as a patient who had run out of options. That meant the doctor had no more to offer. Sam saw himself as a person in distress. He just wanted some understanding and a little guidance. What if the doctor had seen Sam in the same light? Would there have been a different outcome? The sad part is, I'm sure the doctor was not aware of any of this happening even though Sam was under his care.

I can happily say that all over the country there are cancer rehabilitation programs being set up in hospitals to help patients with counseling–from pre-diagnosis throughout the process and are ready with available treatment plans. The goal is to show patients things they can do to help themselves and even support the patient after treatments are done. If you are diagnosed with cancer, search your area, there are an ample amount of options nationwide. You may be able to get the extra help Sam never did.

Another option is to look for a newer model of integrative medicine. There are many practices popping up all over the country. They have a board-certified general practitioner, along with certified naturopaths, chiropractors, acupuncturists, and so forth all under one roof, working together. This helps you get the best of Western and

Alternative medicine. The more you demand these programs and practices as a society, the more society will provide them for you.

My hope for you reading this book is it will start to awaken a deeper part of you that will help you to learn how you are equally as important as what medicine you choose. Learning to balance your Body, Mind, and Spirit and getting to know what weakens your health such as nutrition, stress, environment, and even lack of self- awareness and acting on it as needed, you will be able to build yourself a strong foundation for healing. You will also have an ongoing awareness to what choices will suit you best for whatever you are looking for in your personal healing.

As for the detox program and the case worker overseeing Sam's case, I am short on words to describe the misery this person created in Sam's life. He played on Sam's desperation and the saddest part is I am sure he genuinely believed he was giving Sam solid advice. I don't think such practices are an acceptable form of Alternative medicine, but that's the problem. Without both modalities working together, it's very difficult for the consumer to understand really what is acceptable and what is not.

It bears repeating desperate people do desperate things. It is my contention that if doctors treated the whole person, not just the symptom or illness, they would see this with clarity. As for Sam's role in his own fate, I don't know. Is there a way you can prepare yourself for a terminal diagnosis? Sam had to leave it up to his family to help guide him as best they could. Family can help, but if the patient is unwilling to accept this assistance, they can only help so much. Some people handle their decisions well. They get very organized and map everything out. Others get depressed, go off the deep end, and make extreme choices. One thing is for certain. Sam was a victim of the people he relied on for help. He got different answers from his doctors, from Alternative practitioners, and from his church. Furthermore, he wasn't in a good place inside himself *before* he was diagnosed with cancer. Therefore, he didn't have the balance to navigate all the information coming his way.

One of the many things I learned from Sam is one of the ways to help prepare ourselves for death or a terminal diagnosis is with childhood education in the home as well as in science class. We need to not only discuss the anatomy and physiology of the human body in grade schools, but also the natural process of death and dying from a science perspective and how it happens to all of us, sometimes naturally, sometimes illness, and sometimes tragically. Then maybe we might understand it a little better and fear it a little less. We leave all the questions about death to religion and churches, but it is a natural process that we will all succumb to one day and be exposed to at any given moment. Why is it the one thing we choose not to talk about? The other thing I learned about Sam is how much we fear ourselves and the innate abilities we all must aid in our own healing. Somehow, we went from very little medicine and having to help ourselves to giving all the power to a person who says he or she has our answer. This is our opportunity to start to wake up and become aware of the unlimited healing potential we all have inside.

Sam just wanted to live. But instead of navigating the process, Sam became a victim of it. He should have been focused on living and enjoying his family. I believe, in my heart, that if Sam had taken the time in his life to learn about himself and get acquainted with *The Body Within*, he would have had more tools to help himself. His intuition, instead of his fear, would have guided him. I know Sam is now at peace. I hope writing this will give his struggle some meaning. I feel the best lesson you can learn from Sam's story is how to handle life. That is, how to be secure in who you are, so when adversity hits, you will have the confidence to make difficult decisions. If you can't make life decisions when you're healthy, how do you expect to make them when the chips are down? This leaves you at the mercy of others. Think about it. Who in your life do you really trust to help guide you in making the tough decisions? Some of you are fortunate enough to have someone, but, sadly, many people do not.

This whole journey is about finding balance, intuition, and clarity. With that, you will be able to make solid life choices, career choices, healthcare choices, and maybe even choose when and how you die.

"Chaos Breeds Chaos,
Balance Breeds Peace"
-Marie Knoetig

The Body Within

CHAPTER 7

Trusting My Intuition

THERE I WAS, SITTING in the Intensive Care Unit waiting room with my family: my mother, my oldest brother, two of my sisters and my youngest brother. The energy in the room was filled with confusion and utter disbelief. I looked around the room and wondered: Do I tell them? What do I tell them? How do I tell them? Do I really know anything at all?

Let's rewind to about ten weeks earlier. I was working in an office with several different types of holistic practitioners. There was me—Healing Arts Practitioner, a massage therapist, a physical therapist, an acupuncturist, a chiropractor, and now the newest addition, a psychic. The owner decided to bring in a psychic to join our co-op, and she asked that everyone get a reading so that they could refer clients to her. We were a co-op, so I had decided to stay open to the idea and check it out.

Personally, I'd never been to a psychic. I really did not understand what they did or how they got their information. In my work, I try to empower people to know themselves and use their own intuition to help themselves heal. I am also able to help clear their energy so that they can see more possibilities in their healing and themselves. Sometimes I do know answers, but I like to think of them as possibilities.

This psychic thing was way out of my league. Nevertheless, I sat patiently as she shuffled her cards and made her predictions. This tiny, middle-aged woman had an easygoing personality and a soft voice. I smirked when she said my brother and his wife were headed for a divorce, and there would be a fight over the child. She also told me I was going to need a household repair in a corner of my home. "It's a little expensive," she warned, "so prepare yourself." She went on to tell me a couple more things, including how I would relocate my office to a white house.

Then, snapped the card to the table. She said in a matter-of-fact voice, "Your dad is going to become ill, be admitted to the hospital, and get sent home. After being sent home, he was going to be rushed back a couple of hours later, and he wouldn't survive." What could anyone say to that? My reaction was, "Yeah, right!" None of her predictions seemed plausible, so I just filed them in my memory and continued with life.

A week later, my brother called to say that he and his long-time girlfriend broke up, and they were fighting over the dog. (The psychic was close.)

A couple of weeks after that, I was on my hands and knees, cleaning a corner on the kitchen floor for the new refrigerator. Again, she had been right.

Then, quite unexpectedly, I found my own office space not far from my current one. I would now be working on the second floor of an old Victorian house. You guessed it—white. I gave each event a little nod, remembering what she said, but I really didn't think much about the rest of the reading.

Then, I got a phone call. My dad was in the ER. That evening, he was admitted to the hospital with a bleeding ulcer. At the time, I didn't make the connection. After about three days, the hospital released him. He was only home a few hours when my mom called to say he was in an ambulance being rushed back to the hospital. Only then, did I remember what the psychic said?

There we were, once again, gathered in the ER waiting room. The doctor came in to talk myself and the rest of my family, he said, "Your father has lost many pints of blood, and he is in a coma. He was being transferred to ICU to be stabilized for surgery if they could do surgery at all. It did not look good. We do not think he will survive."

I was stunned, not only because he was going to die but because the psychic said he was going to die. I had a long talk with my closest brother, who is also very intuitive, and he agreed with the psychic. He had been feeling the same thing for a while. I was confused and overwhelmed. How could she know this? How could my brother know? Why didn't I know? What do I do now? I did my best to comfort my mom, while my siblings assured her that Dad was going to be fine. Should I prepare her? Say nothing? What should I do? I couldn't say he was going to be fine. I didn't know if I believed it. Yet, I didn't feel he was going to die either. I was just numb. I distanced myself and took a seat in the corner of the room. I screamed in my head, "What should I do?"

It was as if someone in my head started talking to me, and I heard, "What would you do if you didn't know the outcome?" The voice kept repeating this question over and over until I understood. I smiled and thought, I would do what I always do when someone is in trouble, which is sitting quietly and working on their energy remotely.

When I work on someone's energy remotely – whether they are in the next room or the next state – I sit quietly and focus on their energy or *The Body Within*. As soon as I feel a connection, I allow myself to be guided into doing whatever their energy asks for. It is never the same for any two people. As I hold energetic space for them, their soul's energy uses the space to help them help themselves to create possibilities in their healing, similar to what happened with Grace. They choose what they need, whether it's to heal physically, emotionally, or in my dad's case, to maybe help him pass on. I am a facilitator of the person's journey. I cannot create the outcome I want or what others want. I help the individual help themselves.

Back in the ICU waiting room, I panicked at first, and asked myself, "If I start working on his energy, and feel him dying, then what?" "Well," I answered to myself, "I guess I'll help him die." I had done it for strangers, why not him? I pulled myself together, found a quiet corner, and got to work. After about five minutes, I felt him working to ground his energy and heal the damaged areas in his stomach. I was shocked. He continued healing himself, and I felt he was going to be okay. I looked at my brother and said quietly, "He's going to be okay." He just shook his head and thought I was crazy.

A little later, the doctor came in and said when they went in to stop the bleeding, it had already stopped. They re-cauterized and told us that if he made it through the night, he might have a chance. This was ten years ago. A couple of closer calls, but my dad is still with us.

The takeaway from this story is that a lot of people look to psychics, mediums, and so forth for answers. These individuals may very well be able to read the possibilities in your energy at the time you're sitting across from them. However, as soon as you get up and leave, you still have the power of choice. If you act based on what a psychic says, he or she will influence your journey, and ultimately, head you in the direction of their predictions. This will alter your journey's direction and limit the possibilities in your future choices.

It's all about choice. Make choices for your specific journey without the influence of others' beliefs. When you stop and think about it, how is a psychic any different from parents, teachers, clergy, or society who believe they know what is right for you? The question you need to ask is, "What do I truly know at a deeper level of myself? What is right for me, not anyone else?" This journey is about energy and growth. In order to grow your energy, you need to make choices that benefit you. If someone else gives you the outcome--you didn't choose it--you didn't actually remove any of the blueprints (innate negative behaviors) or negative energy from your space. I will discuss this further in Chapter 9. When you make the choice, you empower yourself and your energy. It is about waking up the healing power you lost long ago.

In this situation, I was creating a stronger connection to *The Body Within*, which was helping me to become more confident every day. As a result, I was able to put myself out there to help someone close to me. I was able to find clarity versus stay caught in the emotional state I was in. If I fed into the psychic's prediction, the outcome would have been negative for my dad, as well as for me, and my personal growth. What I want you to understand is that only you are the master of you! Only you can create the direction your life heads in.

Sue needed to learn just that. Sue was in her early thirties, had a professional job, loved traveling, nice clothes, jewelry, big city living, and so forth. Her family kept pressuring her to get married and have children. Sue didn't feel this was right for her, but she wasn't confident enough to know she could choose not to marry and have kids. She figured it's just what you're supposed to do.

Sue went to a psychic. He told her she was going to meet Mr. Right in three months, and they would marry shortly thereafter. Sue was very excited; now her mom would leave her alone. When I saw her two months after the reading, she was getting very anxious about not meeting him yet. I cautioned Sue that it doesn't happen this way. "You need to be careful not to create it," I told her, "and just let life play out."

Well, at two months and three weeks, Cupid struck. Sue was at a yoga class, the instructor smiled at her, and now it was love-at-first sight. Ken was very spiritual and open to new experiences. However, he had very little financial means and was committed to his basic lifestyle. Sue: fancy, fast life; Ken: comfortable, simple existence. A match made in heaven?

Sue and Ken married about ten months after meeting along with Sue committing to Ken's lifestyle to make him happy. On their first wedding anniversary, Sue woke up from her created reality to see she had simplified her life, not because Ken asked her to, but because she thought she had to. Sue was independent and strong until her traditional blueprints came back to bite her in the toosh. Now, she was working in the same job but had changed the rest of her life to her husband's beliefs and the beliefs of her parents. Gone were the big house, the fancy clothes, makeup, and fun car. Sue realized how much she missed her old life, and how it really was who she was inside.

Fortunately, Ken truly was a spiritual person, and he only wanted for Sue what she wanted for herself. Eventually, Sue was able to move forward and claim her life back. It was Sue's lack of self-confidence that made her susceptible to the psychic's prediction. I'd like to think this experience taught Sue that it was okay to like her life, not the one her family felt was right. But I am not sure that is what happened. Sometimes you repeat the same mistakes repeatedly, and then you finally realize that is a mistake. Once you have this realization, you discover you. Many times, however, people don't recognize the mistake or do recognize that it's a mistake but are afraid to make the changes in themselves to not make it again, so they continue on the same path. I hope Sue figures it out much sooner than later.

These two vastly different psychic experiences have one thing in common. Both demonstrate just how dangerous it is for someone else to map out your future for you. I can't say this enough, so you're going to hear it again and again: Choices, choices, choices! They're yours, not someone else's. Failing to make a choice could cost you as little as a traffic ticket, or, as you saw with me, it could have cost my dad his opportunity to heal and me my personal growth.

This is why tapping into *The Body Within* is so important. The more you connect with your intuition, you will have the confidence to make these choices without the need for someone else to tell you whether you are right or wrong. Your intuition is always there for you; you just have to find a balance to hear it.

With that said, whenever anyone takes away your power of choice, it weakens your energy—it weakens you. Decide what you want, how you want it, and make things happen. Will it always be the right choice? If it teaches you something about yourself – whether you like something or not, whether you're good at something or not - then, yes, it's the right choice. As long as you're the one making the choice, it's always right. When the next decision comes along, you'll have tools and a history to guide you, if you choose to be open and aware. There's no right or wrong answer; there's only learning who you are.

CHAPTER 8

What Are You Looking for from Medicine?

HOW DID WE GET from biting bullets in a battlefield during the Civil War, having to do whatever we could to figure out to help ourselves in order to not die from an infection or viruses, delivering our babies at home, to now expecting a practitioner to know us better than we know ourselves?

Pam is a 35-year-old female who had been to many practitioners over the years for chronic fatigue and chronic pain issues. Her chief complaints were that she tried to exercise, but it would exhaust her and cause more pain. By the end of her day, she had nothing left physically or emotionally, had chronic headaches with neck and shoulder pain. Her Western doctors told her all her test results were normal and that nothing was wrong. She went the Alternative route, and they diagnosed her with mental toxicity/adrenal failure and Lyme disease. She was on so many supplements and large doses of antibiotics, but nothing seemed to work to help her regain her health. She came in and I worked with *The Body Within* and was able to see a lower right belly scar and she explained she had her appendix removed 20 years prior. This caused her right hip to be internally rotated and lack of push off from the toes to the hip. Then on her left side, her spleen and her ribcage and all the surrounding tissue and fascia were stuck, so there was no internal torso rotation as she walked. Instead of her core moving when she walked, her body moved as one piece instead of in segments. Her muscles in her back were very limited in movement, and she no longer had any signs of her natural movements in her back, torso, and arms. There were no signs of the movement she was born with. I asked if she had ever had mono as this is typical of many who have had a serious case of it. And she had had it when she was 14.

I worked with her energy and was able to help her body release the spleen and some of the right lower belly scarring. The problem with old injuries is sometimes the body protects so much during the incident that it never returns to normal after it has healed. Then the body heals and just goes on as if nothing happened, not even realizing it still has limitations. Tapping into *The Body Within* and listening to the cues her body gave me, the body released what was no longer serving her from that time.

As soon as we did that, her belly area and mid-lower back started to relax. We were able to help her regain some internal torso rotation, and within a few days, her energy levels started to improve. Her headaches and neck and shoulder pain began to dissipate. I explained to her she was going to have to start to listen to her body, start stretching daily, learn about using a roller to soften some of the back muscles and focus on learning how to wake up her core muscles by going to a physical therapist, working with a personal trainer or self-teaching by reading or watching videos along with information that I had supplied her. Her work had just begun, but a new life was on the horizon. As we continued to work together, in each session we found areas of the body that were not moving correctly and causing her physical stress as the body had found new patterns around the old injuries. We released those and I sent her off with basic core exercises to wake up the body to its innate way of moving. Some sessions included intuitive body work while other sessions I focused in on stress or nutrition. I found her body was too tired to do any physical healing which alerted me to questions on what could be weakening her body. and I questioned her--it was tired from the poor nutrition and the stress she was under. This meant to me the body was locking down in survival mode to preserve versus heal. As time went on, her healing went from getting better and stronger each session to going to a slow crawl. Her attitude toward her healing was deteriorating because the more she read about the extensive issues you could have with your hormones, your thyroid, your adrenals she got off track. She read about all the extensive blood work, medicines, supplements, and herbs available to her, so she started back on her path from practitioner to practitioner. She was taking more supplements and sometimes more meds. She continued to see me on a limited basis but not doing any of the work we had started. I watched her frustration hoping someone had the answer, spending so much time and money, more diet limitations, and still feeling even more miserable with more aches and pains. The more I pushed the memory of the progress we had achieved, the more she pushed back. She wanted a quick fix—she wanted a pill or some other fast treatment. In other words, she didn't want to do the work. I sat her down and broke it to her gently, "You are putting in so much time and energy anyway—in travel time, testing time, work time to pay for all of this, research time, time away from the things you love because you are struggling with pain and not feeling well. Your life had drastically improved when you were working with me. Yes, we did not have a quick answer but every day you saw improvement. You need to understand that medicine can test for a lot of things but life can damage the body equally as a hormone" She looked at me in the eyes and replied, "Someone must have THE answer, it can't be on my shoulders. What if I am missing that one thing that could cure me?

As has happened many times before, I replied, "Medicine is a tool that constantly changes and its answers' change as the science changes. It will never have all the answers, so it's crucial that you become part of that answer by knowing yourself and past injuries, lifestyle weaknesses like poor nutrition, too much stress, not exercising, etc. Your long-term health and wellness depend on it." She still did not like it, but it got her back to focusing on her for a few months, and her health improved again. And again, as happens so often, she got tired and went back to look for that magic bullet.

Mark is a 58-year-old male with chronic pain and an endless determination to fix it. After exhausting all resources on the Western medicine side, he started on his journey to get someone to fix him on the Alternative medicine side.

I met Mark four or five years into his journey of looking for the one cure for all his ailments. Mark was a tall, muscular, hard-working physical laborer who had many physical injuries. He had tried homeopathy, which supplied many reasons for his pain, none of them muscular skeletal. He tried a naturopath and again had been given many reasons. He was using a chiropractor, a massage therapist, someone who specialized in Rolfing, Electro Muscle Stimulation, Alexander Technique, MAP, you name it, and if it existed, he was trying it. Each time, the practitioner had the answer 'they were going to fix him'. I met him midway through his journey and after working with him and his history, I knew he was always pushing his body to the max. He had surgery for many injuries that had affected the normal gait pattern of his body even after the surgeries his body could not regain normal function, along with general issues that stressed his body as well. His body had adjusted to the trauma, and genetic issues he had but living in this body was causing pain and discomfort that he did not want to deal with. I explained, "We can work with your limitations and help you become the best you, decrease your pain levels enormously, but there is no real fix to get you back the perfect body. You will always have to work at it to stay out of pain. You will also have to be present, and you must be willing to take 'me time' every day to make this happen. You can be the best you can be, but you will never be like you were in your twenties or thirties."

According to him, I just had no clue what I was talking about because everyone he would meet would tell him otherwise. I have watched this man spend thousands of dollars fighting a reality that is unchangeable. Do I believe people can heal themselves? Of course, but healing comes in many packages. Marks healing was for him to realize his limitations and accept them so he can regain his quality of life and manage his pain rather than fight a reality he can never change.

Alice taught me a long time ago that healing comes from within but once the body is missing its original parts or altered surgically in a way that the body can only adapt, you will always have to mindful of how you feel and the stress you put on yourself in order to make sure you stay strong and balanced. I had met Alice when she was in her late 70s, she was blind in her left eye since she was a child and had cataract surgery on her right. Unfortunately, her eyesight was altered during the surgery and now her right eye was failing. She wanted my help. She wanted me to fix her right eye so she could hold on to her eyesight. She never told me which eye was bad, just wanted my help. As I proceeded to work on her, I went right to the left eye. She got mad and told me it was her right eye that needed fixing— the left had been blind since she was a child. Now I'm curious. I focus my intent on the right, but I can't see the energy and the body is not giving me any clues on how to help. I could get the energy to focus on healing the left eye. Her body did not know how or what to do with the right eye.

She was terribly upset with me, but I knew at that moment how smart her body was. It can work to heal what it knows innately, the left eye, but anything that has been altered with surgery, her right eye, a hip replacement, or knee replacement, etc. I can help your body adapt to them but not completely accept them as the norm. What I did learn is that if all our working parts are there, the possibilities in healing are endless. This helped me with my work and has given me a deeper understanding of the level of healing the body can accomplish. Unfortunately, Alice did not let me try to work with her left eye so we will never know if it was possible to help heal it.

Paul is a 45-year-old marathon runner. He had a pulled hamstring that did not want to heal. I explained that he needs to take running back a step and work to regain his body's natural gait. His back, neck, and shoulders no longer had a natural swing or movement. His scapula's (or wing bones as people know them), were tight and not propelling his body forward when he ran. He had to do that himself, which was putting extra stress on many other parts of the body, along with his thoracic spine. With his back so tight, he couldn't stretch his lower body properly, so unless he corrected the problem, he would Band Aid the hamstring, leading to bigger problems. He declined my advice, "My back is fine," and was not going to break his training because the shoulders have nothing to do with the hamstrings' stretching. He was not a world class runner; he was not breaking any records except for his own. He would not disappoint friends or family if he waited till the next race to get his body back. He was competing against himself. He was the only one he was going to let down. I could repeat this scenario many times with athletes who have come to see me through the years.

When you are pushing your body past its limits, you not only override your nervous system into fooling the body to do what it does not feel is in your best interest, you also train your mind that anything is possible. I talk about endless possibilities in your healing, but anything is possible is very different than taking advantage of the endless possibilities available to use for creating health, wellness and aging gracefully. People in chronic pain don't want to move because it hurts and they are not aware enough to know there is good pain and that sometimes you have to push the body to remember what it has forgotten. That is why tapping into your Body Within is crucial. Some people have never put any time or energy into their health, so they have no concept how to read their body to learn what changes need to be made to lessen the stress so it can heal. Extreme athletes won't slow down because they can't tell the difference between good pain and bad pain, and they have an agenda. Unfortunately, they have pushed past the warning signs their body is giving them that basically says: enough is enough. I wonder what will happen when they have an illness. Will they be aware, or will they not be able to hear that either? I fear it is the latter.

As a society, we have developed a narrow focus on what healthy really is between how much we weigh, how we look, how many dead lifts we can do, etc. Health is so much more, that is what this book is about. *The Body Within* is the key to help you to know if you are at the ideal weight for your body if you are exercising enough of too much, is your job causing you age quickly, is your nutrition stressing your body, etc. You can go from practitioner to practitioner in hopes for all the answers and an easy cure but most, if not all, healing starts with you. Your practitioner doesn't live in your skin, does not know your stress, eat with you, or go to the grocery store with you. They do not see if you cook or do take out all the time. They don't know if your couch is old and killing your back. They don't know if your exercise is helping or hurting you. They don't know about your job. They have no idea that you sit at the computer all day and don't do anything to offset that wear and tear in your body. They have no idea if you fight with your spouse or your teenager is stressing you, adding to your body's wear and tear. They don't know if your old injuries are causing stress on your body now. I could go on. All they know is that you do not feel well, and they have a limited amount of time with you. They order a test to see if they can pinpoint the problem and try to find ways to quantify how to help you, not how you can help yourself. When dealing with chronic pain and overall health and wellness, the rest, my friend, is up to you.

I want to encourage YOU to learn to get in touch with *The Body Within* and check in with YOUR body, mind, and spirit every day, work with the bedtime routine Chapter 9. It will alert you to things that are draining your health; it's up to you to listen. Put the intent out and really ask, what do I need to see to stimulate healing, and my long-term health and wellness.

The Body Within

CHAPTER 9

Healing and Energy

THERE IS A DIRECT CORRELCATION between healing and keeping yourself in balance. We've seen how those two factors: healing and balance were not practiced by Sam and Mary. I am sure that if they had practiced these two important systems things could have turned out differently for them. And of course, the real question is: Is there anything you can do to prevent you from ever being in Sam and Mary's shoes? To answer that question, you need to delve deeper into how you heal. What is this ultimate journey you're on, and how do your decisions dictate whether or not you're living your life to your full potential?

Why did Sam, from Chapter 6, develop cancer? And why was Mary, Chapter 5, afflicted with all those health issues? Did they have a choice or did these bad circumstances simply happen to them? Let us start with energy anatomy. I see you as a Body, Mind, and Spirit. The body is your temple. The mind is the brains of the operation. The spirit or soul (what I call *The Body Within*) is the conscience, the part of you that is connected to the universe. What does any of this have to do with your health? Everything! I believe that balancing all three is the key. We talked about balance earlier, but now you're going to learn *how* to balance, and what balance truly means to your quality of life.

If you have researched energy medicine, then you've probably heard or read about yin and yang, chakras, meridians, outer layers and inner layers, and so forth. I really have no opinion on these spiritual theories. What I'm absolutely certain of, however, is that total healing is much more personal and goes deeper than you may realize.

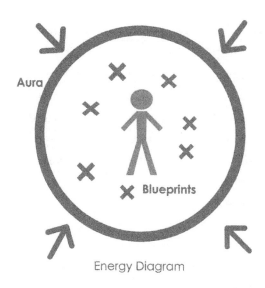

Energy Diagram

Let's start by looking at the diagram above. This is my representation of your energy anatomy, not your physical self. Imagine you're the person in the center. That's *The Body Within*, the true you without blinders; when you are at your best, not jaded by life, beliefs, fear grief, anger, greed, etc. The circle of energy around you is your aura. Think of it as your own personal bubble. This energy bubble is your protection from the outside world. It is your own magic shield. Have you ever walked into a room and known someone was having a bad day even before they opened their mouth? You sensed whether they were happy or sad just by standing next to them. That's their aura, or energy, hitting yours. Some people are better than others at reading people's energy or aura. Most husbands get grief because they're not very good at it. Moms tend to be really good at it. They have the ability to tell if something is wrong without being told.

If you're adept at reading someone's aura, it can be a very useful tool to warn you when to watch what you say. By the same token, it can also tell you if it's an optimal time to let it rip. Your aura can be very strong to protect you from other people's energy. What makes it strong is self-confidence, living in a world without blinders, and a strong connection to yourself. Your aura can also be very weak and pliable, which can make you extra sensitive and out of balance. What makes it weak is a lack of self-confidence, living in a created reality, and reliance on others to choose for you. Being out of balance can weaken you physically and emotionally. So, knowing that you can work on it and police it daily is a great benefit. That is why it is so important to learn about *The Body Within*. The more you connect to it, the more you can become aware of your weaknesses, and you can correct them yourself.

Inside your aura you have, what I refer to as, blueprints. (This is only my interpretation, it's an infinite universe.) You get these blue- prints from your parents, teachers, society, and even the energy you grow up in. They are passed down from their parents, society, and so on. This may be the reason why you hate snakes, and so does Dad and Grandma, but not one of you has ever met a snake to really have any opinion about it. These blueprints are behaviors, beliefs, food preferences, and so forth. Now, let's add into that space everything you've learned since you were born. That is, everything you were told about how life works.

This includes, but is not limited to, religion, politics, money attitudes, diet, even how to dress. Add in everything teachers, doctors, clergy, parents, and others have taught you with since you came into this world. All these things make up what I call the muck or blue- prints in your energy. Also, it's not just what they taught you; it's how you <u>interpreted</u> what they taught you. You know how you can say one thing, pass it around a room, and everyone has a different interpretation.

This is especially true of children. How they hear — how they interpret - what we tell them. Their interpretations of what we tell them as a child carry with them through life till something clicks to help them see it is wrong. Then they have a choice to change how they see it. The best way to avoid this is to talk about life with children and explain what you mean when you say it. It is different for every age, but the older children are, the more they should know. They should have a clear understanding rather than come up with their own conclusion. Here's a simple example of a child's interpretation and how it could have gone one way or the other. When my grandson was about three years old, he loved *The Wizard of Oz*. Auntie Julie gave Zack a pop-up book of all the characters and sat with him to look at the book. She gathered him to her side, and together they opened the book. Zack snuggled up to her, and squeaked with delight, pointing to each character on the first page.

Sarah asked, "Zack, who is your favorite character?" With a giggle, Zack answered, "The witch." Julie said, "Oh, you like Glinda, the good witch?" Zack replied, "No, I like the bad witch." Zack's mom, Janet and Auntie Julie then chimed in together. "Zack, you like Glinda, the good witch, right?" By then Zack was very clear as he insisted, he liked the bad witch. Janet and Julie continued to persist in convincing Zack that he must be mistaken, and, in fact, he must really like the good witch. They were clearly troubled, thinking he liked bad (not good) and they were going to try to change his mind.

I joined in and asked, "So Zack, you like the bad witch?" His eyes lit up. "Yes, Grammy, I like the bad witch." Janet and Julie rolled their eyes. "Why do you like the bad witch?" I asked. Wide-eyed and excited, Zack exclaimed, "Cuz she's green!" Now, it was my turn to roll my eyes. If Janet and Julie had convinced Zack that he really liked Glinda, would Zack have ended up hating bad witches or perhaps the color green (or them)? That is what I interpret as muck in your energy, distorted understanding of how life actually is.

As a child, how did you interpret what was said to you by your parents, teachers, society, and so forth, and how do your own kids interpret what you tell them? We know what we mean, but does it match up with their interpretation? Kids will often just agree with what you say and come up with their own interpretation. Maybe a week, a month, a year, or even ten years later, they figure out that their interpretation (the muck in their energy) was wrong all along. When that moment happens, their energy shifts, and a blueprint dissolves. We call that an awakening. When that happens, it helps to balance your Body, Mind, and Spirit a bit more to create more peace and more energy to put toward your healing.

Now look to the outside of your aura in the diagram above. That's all the information coming to you from the universe, or God, or Wakan Tankan, or Buddha, and so forth. (I'm not here to say which-- that's your journey.) That's your intuition. It's how you know someone needs something before they ask; how you know something is canceled before you get the call, or how you know someone is sick before they get a diagnosis. It could be, we all know things but there's no rational reason to know them—this is the intuition piece. That is, there's no logical explanation for why we know certain things we do. But the truth is, everything you need to know in life is all there waiting for you. But how can that be if you can't hear it?

You can't hear it because your energy is filled with all the blue- prints and muck you've acquired since childhood. Blueprints and muck are everything you <u>believe</u> to be true, not what really is. It's like shining a flashlight through a very thick, smoky room. The light is your intuition, the smoke is your muck. Hence, only a few rays of light can get through.

Having intuition does not make you a gifted person. Everyone has it. It does not make you a chosen one, and it certainly doesn't give you special powers above anyone else. What intuition does is helps make you a balanced, healthy, aware, stress-free, happy person. Some people call themselves gifted when they know things others don't. It just means they're more open in some areas of their energy than others, not necessarily balanced. Here's why: being balanced will help you to be open in all three areas – Body, Mind, Spirit - not just one. The more you learn to balance your energy, the more you will hear your intuition (*The Body Within* talking to you.) The more you listen, the easier life becomes because you are no longer fighting a dictated reality. That's saying "It is what it is" there's a lot of power in those words. You will be living in what is.

With my own healing, I find that every time I learn how to see situations in a new light and learn to direct my thoughts and actions with more understanding, my energy gets a little lighter, and my body heals a little more. Plus, my intuition gets even stronger. There is no magic bullet. It's about you healing you, and waking up from your distorted reality. The clearer your reality, the clearer your energy.

I can hear a lot of minds thinking she's crazy! I live in reality! My answer to that is: everyone lives in what they believe life to be, not necessarily what life is at that moment in time. If you can slow down enough to be truly present, you will start to see how you probably live more in reaction than you do in action.

You were taught at a young age that things happen a certain way. That stops you from seeing how things are happening because you already know. It's just like tying your shoes. Do you ever stop to see how you tie them? Or do you just do it without thinking? So many questions, so little time.

A big step in your awakening occurs when you become a teenager. This is when you start your journey. Parents, teachers, clergy, and others often dread these years. It's when you start to question what people have taught you and ask yourself: Does it make sense? This is when parents have a choice. Do you listen to your kids, even if it seems more like rebellion, or do you blow off their questions and opinions altogether because it's not what you think or believe? This is where intuition comes in.

The more productive, healthier approach is for parents to determine if their kids are unrealistic in their new thinking. Maybe Mom and Dad want their kids to follow the rules because they feel they are the parents and are right. That's when parents should pause and ask themselves: Do my rules make sense? Why am I asking this of them?

Am I teaching my kids to think like me or think for themselves?" It's possible you're both off-track, and there's a different solution.

Here's an example. A client of mine, Laurie, a woman in her 50s, slightly overweight, a librarian, came in one day and went on and on about her daughter, Sara. Sara, around 24 years old, wouldn't listen. Laurie and her husband tried and tried, but Sara kept making mistakes and wouldn't do what they said. I said to Laurie, "So, what you're saying is you want Sara to live her life the way you and your husband do because that's the way you're supposed to?" Laurie answered "Well, yes."

I started laughing and asked Laurie, "So, are you really happy with your life and the way it turned out?" She conceded, "Well, no." Yet Laurie still wanted her daughter to live the way she did. Who's the smarter one here? Is it Sara for trying to find a better way without help from her parents and that's why she is making so many mistakes? Or Laurie, for trying to lead her daughter down the same path?

How do you think Laurie leading Sara down a path that is not of her choosing would work out? Isn't that when we become our parents? Isn't Sara doing what she is supposed to do, making choices to try to figure out what's right for her? Why, as parents, do we think we know what's best for our kids when they're grownups? Do we think like them? Do they think like us? Do they have the same personality or talents? If not, then how can they make the same choices we make?

We all do it on some level. We have standards we live by. The key is to catch ourselves, to realize when it becomes less about a foundation and more about directing others to what you feel is best for them. As soon as you become aware of your actions or your tunnel vision, you can choose to change it, this will take time, but is worth it. (Enjoy the journey.) As soon as you change it, you get rid of some of that muck in your energy and in theirs. The reward: more intuition and clarity comes into your life and the lives of your children, and you heal yourself in many ways. Sometimes emotionally, sometimes physically, and sometimes it helps you create balance to help you connect to *The Body Within* more clearly.

What is the most common culprit when it comes to blockages in your energy? Beliefs. Beliefs in religion, lifestyle, even choices in medicine. Why? It's the fear that surrounds these issues, not the issues themselves. What if I question? What if I am wrong? Society has imposed such severe consequences if you choose to question these issues, it becomes a lot safer to hold on to your familiar (but often limiting) beliefs and fight them to the death.

You restrict yourself with your fears and you don't even realize you're doing it. When someone asks you about religion, lifestyle, or Alternative versus Western medicine, do you feel a defensive wall immediately go up? Especially if it goes against what you know to be true? Before that wall goes up, maybe there is a split second of awareness when you say to yourself 'Gee, maybe I should question what I think to be true. Maybe I should look into this further.' At that moment, you <u>should</u> investigate it further. Most times there is no awareness because these issues have been with you since birth. Who knows how you interpreted them as a child. Maybe visiting them will help you see them clearer and even teach you wonderful things you never heard when you were a child. All the energy around these issues is, what I call, the foundation of who you are. If you rock the foundation, then you have no strength. Think about when someone asks you about any of these issues, how do you feel?

If you feel defensive, ask yourself: Why do I need to grasp on so tightly to my beliefs? If it's a truth and not just belief, do you really need to hold on to it or is it just there? A belief you fight for can be as weighty as differences in religious beliefs to how to cook and eat spaghetti. Are you defensive because you believe in your truth so strongly you couldn't possibly be wrong? How can yours be right and all the other versions be wrong? Is that like hitting the Megabucks from birth? You were lucky enough to buy the winning ticket of knowledge! This is often the cause of blockages in someone's energy

… the internal struggle, the nagging question: "What if I'm wrong?"

The good news is that as soon as you have that split second of awareness and realize you might be wrong; it creates a little glimpse of light shining through. The purpose of this glimpse is to help you see more light. This, in turn, creates more space in your energy to help you sensing more possibilities coming through. However, that does not mean it will change how you feel about these issues. What it will do is help you see if it is your own truth or the truth of others that were imposed on you in your youth. Once it becomes your truth, it clears your energy. It's like this, if I go to the doctor, and he gives me medicine for my illness, and I take it simply because he's the doctor and he knows better, then I create muck in my aura. If I go to the doctor and discuss the medicine, research it, and take it because I feel it's what I need, according to all the information, a big piece of muck leaves my energy. Same answer, simply different energy behind it and you are stronger in who you are, having made the choice yourself, not someone else making it for you. All it takes is a moment to acknowledge the light, consider the new idea and things start to shift.

As you learn how you process information, you may realize you use the knowledge that you gain and spin it to keep you safe according to the weaknesses you have inside. That is what makes you create your own reality, rather than seeing the reality around you.

I had a friend of a friend who claimed to be an enlightened being. He told me that I could never be enlightened unless I learned the way he learned or learned from the people who taught him. I just smiled. What else could I say or do? Who said I was enlightened? Why did he think I was? Who said he was? In his reality, he was right, and you could only learn from his way. It's a big universe with lots of teachers. How did he get so lucky to find the only one?

There are all kinds of reasons for energy blockages, some of them quite foolish. Here's a personal example, and one of my favorites. My husband and I ride motorcycles. Carl rides a Harley. I don't. When I first started riding, Carl told me the Rules of Riding and they are as follows:

The only real bike is a Harley. When we're out riding and anyone waves, they're waving at him – on the Harley. Harley people only wave to Harley people. (I call this the Harley religion.) Every time we go out with friends, the Harley riders gather to look at each other's bikes. No one even looks at mine because, well, it's not a Harley.

They all have the same aura about them, and you're supposed to dress and act a certain way when riding a Harley. They even have to wear Harley clothes to go to the Harley store. Personally, I'm glad there are so many new bike builders to help these people open their vision a little --- and maybe expand their wardrobe a little, too (wink, wink.)

Now for the awakening. One day about ten years ago, my husband had no choice but to ride my bike. You would think it was the worst thing that ever happened to him. I was on the back. As soon as he started to relax into the ride and enjoy it, I felt his energy shift. A Harley blue- print had just dissolved. Did he admit it? Maybe, a little. Carl's still a diehard Harley guy, but that day he realized there really are other decent bikes sharing the road! After that one little shift, he cleaned some muck and opened his energy to a new way of thinking. This led to more new experiences in other areas of Carl's life. That's how it works. One change can cause a domino effect of change. It's truly amazing once you experience it. When your energy is blocked, you live out of balance and chaos is your strength. Chaos breeds chaos: and any area of your life can be affected: your health, your family, your finances, your friendships, and so forth. Not because the chaos is your punishment or its your karma or the Universe has this planned for you but because you are too chaotic or distracted to see or hear the bus coming, so it hits you. True healing comes from cleaning up the muck and letting *The Body Within* guide you to a greater sense of health, wellness, and healthy aging.

Now that I've explained how and why your energy becomes blocked, I'd like to share some tools to help you clear your energy and open your awareness to more possibilities. Some I have learned along the way, others I gained from intuition and guidance. I find each one works in a different way, so play with them and see if you connect to one or more, or even, intuitively, develop your own. Again, take notes as you read. If this information stirs up an experience or patterns in your own thoughts that you feel you need to work on, take a minute to jot them down.

As you experiment with these tools, choose one to work with at least once a day for a couple of weeks. Give yourself time to process the technique and see if you can start to sense your own energy field. Remember, you are your own energy balancer and cleaner, so take it seriously. The more you practice, the stronger you will become.

Self-healing Hands-On

If you have chronic pain, illness, everyday aches or even an acute injury; lay on your back, close your eyes and picture yourself standing in front of you and see if you can get a sense of your energy body. What you are doing is just picturing an image of yourself facing you. Then see if you can sense it or see a shadow image of yourself. Don't expect it to be what you think, just stay open. Then with open, clear intent, ask to see what you need to see, and see if you become more aware of one part of your body more than any other part.

As soon as your awareness is alerted, see if it is the same spot that you have pain or if it is somewhere different. Sometimes, pain is not always coming from where it hurts.

Then, place one of your hands on the spot you are alerted to and just leave it there with the intent for your body to heal itself. Now as you are holding that spot, see if you have referred pain to a different spot or maybe just feel guided to another spot. If you don't sense anything just put the second hand on your stomach and put your other hand on that area. You might see it in your mind's eye or you might feel it in your body, or you just might get a thought that alerts you to a body part. Don't over think it. Just put out the intention and then let the thought go.

You may feel nothing at all, or you may feel sensations of warmth and tingling. Just relax and allow the body to have the increased focus and awareness to try to create change. Don't judge it, just relax, let your mind wander and then see what happens. Observe versus taking part in it. Do this often so you can work on the correction. The more you focus inward, the stronger The Body Within gets and then directs you.

Quiet Time before Bed

Sleep is the most important thing you can do to keep yourself healthy, balanced, and focused. Many of us have a hard time getting restful sleep, falling asleep, or even waking up. Quiet time before bed is one of the challenges in my challenge book, *The Body Within Wellness Challenge*. It goes into much greater detail. My challenge to you is to take twenty minutes before bed, put on quiet music, lie on the floor, and do basic breathing and stretching exercises. Pay attention to how tight your muscles are and focus on breathing and relaxing.

Start to get to know your body and observe if it is stressed.

Try to learn about what your body feels like at the end of the day. Are your muscles tight? Is your mind racing? Do you want to go to bed for seven hours and bring all that stress with you? You do most of your healing and repairing from your day when sleeping. Do you want to do it with chaos or balance in your body?

Now that you are relaxed, check in on your day. What kind of day did you have? If it was chaotic, what caused it? Are there changes you can make so it can go smoother tomorrow?

Next, check in on your nutrition and exercise. Were you able to meal plan or take the time to make healthy choices? Did you have time to walk or exercise? Did you have goals to meet? Did you meet your goals for the day?

Now, check in with *The Body Within*. Did you have intuition moments that you were aware of? Did *The Body Within* alert you at any time to alter your behavior or make different choices throughout your day? If it did, did you listen? Are you starting to see a bigger picture of how living out of balance can accumulate over time? Did you find you react less when you catch yourself in chaotic behavior?

Breathing

Another energy clearing tool is to work with your breathing. Breath is life. Just lay quiet, sit, or stand – whatever makes you happy - and take long breaths in, and exhale long breaths out. With the breath in, bring in white healing light and on the breath out, exhale all the negativity in your space. Use your mind with strong intent. It will surprise you when you feel lighter after you exhale. Play with it, do it quietly, going slower/faster, or at a normal pace. Most of all, just

Mala Beads

Using mala beads is a good way to start to quiet your thoughts and start to connect to be able to hear *The Body Within*. They are similar to rosary beads used in the Catholic Church. Mala beads are universal prayer beads that help you quiet your mind and train yourself to focus. You can move to each bead with a breath, a mantra, or just hold them while meditating. The challenge is to figure out what works for you.

You can purchase a strand of already-made mala beads on the internet or in gift shops. However, I recommend that you pick out your own beads and make the mala yourself or ask someone to do it for you. Why do I prefer the make-your-own beads strand? Traditional ones are usually made of wooden beads, but I prefer the beads be made of stone, and you should select the stone that's right for you. Stones, rocks, and so forth, are some of the most powerful healing tools you should consider exploring. The rock does not have to be special but can be one you find walking on the beach or trail. Stones all have some natural healing properties, and mixed with your personal energy, they can balance you or mess you up. I find the biggest mistake is letting someone else choose a stone for you. It's best that you pick them out yourself. Don't Google "stones" and just buy what you think might be a good fit. Someone else's opinion isn't better than what your own body can tell you. If you don't want to go with the mala bead route, go for a walk in the woods or at the beach and pick a rock that "feels right." To pick your beads, go to a bead or craft store and look at the display of 8 mm around beads made of natural stone. Before you pick up a strand, get a sense of how you feel inside. Feel yourself grounded to the earth. Then, pick up a bead and hold it. Decide how it makes you feel? Anxious, calm, tired, angry, peaceful? Do this until you find a bead that makes you feel peaceful inside. That's your bead. Do the same thing with rocks you are drawn to and put one in your pocket, on your desk, near your bed, and hold it when you feel unbalanced. They are amazing, I promise.

Now that you have your mala beads, it's time to go online and read some articles about how to use them. Don't just take my word for it -- learn, question, play, and figure out what works for you. If you want to recite a mantra as you go around the beads twice, I highly recommend the one below. If you don't have beads, you can still use the mantra holding a rock or by itself to help clear your energy. I have chosen this mantra for a couple of reasons. First, I gained it intuitively, and it has been a core part of my healing physically, emotionally, and spiritually. Second, I have given it to many of my friends and clients, and it has helped them achieve amazing results as well. Remember, this is only a recommendation, so if you see it differently, by all means, change it to personalize it for your own healing. Here's the mantra:

I am quieting my mind. I
am embracing my soul.
I am open to all possibilities in my healing.

I trust and have faith; I am protected.

I am quieting my mind: This means you are the power within yourself to quiet yourself.

I am embracing my soul: You recognize you have a deeper sense of who you are and are willing to tap into it (*The Body Within*).

I am open to all possibilities in my healing: You are open to seeing all your self-imposed limitations and their roots, no matter what they are.

I trust and have faith, and I am protected: It means you are empowering yourself to believe in yourself and know that you are your own healer and protector. (No one else can be your protector of *The Body Within*. It comes from the internal power that lies in *The Body Within*.) You are your power. You are *The Body Within*.

The key to the mantra is to really mean it as you say it. Words are empty unless you empower them with your intent. See yourself reading the words as you say them. Be careful not to use a specific intent with mantras.

For instance, you want to say, if you're dealing with money: Financial abundance is here. Not: I want to make $100,000/year. Let me caution you when you are using positive affirmations or mantras, you still want to look for the 'signs' along the way that are helping you manifest this. Such as, someone tells you about a job. While it may not have a starting wage that you think is great, ask yourself, should I pursue this? It just may or may not be the steppingstone you are looking for. Be open to what you need, not what you want or what you think you need. Again, if you see the process differently, then by all means, do it differently. Trust there is a reason you see using mala beads your way and figure out what that reason is.

Quiet Sitting

If the mala beads aren't for you, try quiet sitting. I don't mean meditation, which I also find very helpful. I have had people tell me meditation or trying to meditate stresses them out. If you meditate and it works for you, keep it up. If you have tried it and struggled, try this. Find some place that makes you feel good and sit and observe. I like to sit and watch nature. Follow a bird, squirrel, even an ant – that's my favorite. Follow it, watch it, and figure out where it goes. What do you think it looks like down in the hole? Or watch bees collect pollen. It's easy--it helps quiet your mind and brings you peace, but mostly, it's about being present.

Simple Energy Clearing

If you are feeling overwhelmed, tired, or you feel like a cold is coming on, this is a great tool. Stand and put your hands at shoulder height, your elbows bent and horizontal to the ground, fingertips almost touching. Push your hands slowly down the front of your body to the ground. Try to feel the resistance of the energy, or the air, or however you want to perceive it. Do it again and again. It should feel easier each time. Your intent is to push the negative energy that's on you into the earth. Think of this intention as you do it. It will give you more power. You should feel lighter when you're done. Do this

Solar Plexus Clearing

The solar plexus is located on your belly, just below your ribs. Again, whenever you're feeling overwhelmed, stressed, angry, just scoop the energy and throw it away. With your mind, take it and throw it outside of your bubble. It may look silly but works like a charm. When you're driving and feeling stressed, simply scoop and throw. Scoop and throw. Don't feel embarrassed. No one can see you, and you'll prevent road rage. Everyone wins.

Mini Me – Energy Clearing

I find Mini-me to be one of the most powerful healing tools for everyone if you can take it seriously and really work to master it. Sit quietly in a chair. Put a teddy bear on your lap or use your mind to visualize a miniature (mini me) energetic you on your lap. Put both hands over the energetic you or the teddy bear. Close your eyes and ask for guidance. Just say in your mind, "Help me, help myself." Then, wait. You may feel nothing, you may feel pressure on your hands, or your hands may feel like moving. Let them. They may clear or scoop. Let them be guided and notice as you feel it in your hand. You may start to feel it in your body at the same time. Do this daily and you'll see how it gets stronger. The stronger it is, the more tools will emerge from *The Body Within* to help you heal in endless ways. Relax, don't try to be perfect. Just be with it and see what happens. If you can be patient and master this one, I find it to be one of the most powerful self-help healing tools.

Scars and Injury Focus

If you are someone who has had sports injuries, surgeries, car accidents, or just life, start to get to know your body and become more aware of the restrictions and limitations these injuries are causing. This helps your body to wake up to lost functions and patterns that create whole health. Take a past or current injury or limitation and move that area. Maybe it's your ankle, just play with your ankle, stretch it side to side and become aware of how it works. Foam Rolling is a great place to start. There are many books, videos, and articles online about Foam Rolling your tight tissue areas. To get started for the first time, I recommend the book *The Melt Method*. It has a lot of tools to help you help yourself. Then compare it to the opposite side of your body. What do you notice? Do they move the same, stretch the same, and so forth? If not, stretch the tight side, massage it, work with your body to help it remember.

Take the time to massage new and old scars to help loosen scar tissue and soften the injured areas to promote blood flow and healing.

Light Yoga

A lot of people find yoga relaxing, but it also can be physically stressful, especially if done improperly, or if your body has many limitations. The key to yoga is understanding the depth of it. Yoga, like most Eastern philosophies, is a practice. You don't rush, you don't add poses until you can properly do the ones you've learned already. Take the time with each pose to feel your body's strengths and weaknesses and work with them. You practice every day, and you can always improve, but you never perfect it. In our modern-day society, in our quick fix mentality, have taken one of the most successful healing tools and turned it into a fitness competition like everything else.

Yoga should be undertaken slowly and used as a way to not only stretch but to learn total body awareness and presence in your body. If you find yoga comfortable and enjoyable, keep practicing and learning new poses. If yoga is difficult for you, find a good teacher who will approach it slowly and help you succeed. Try not to get frustrated and give up. It's really worth it.

Chi Gong

Chi Gong is an Eastern practice that promotes physical and emotional healing and balancing your energy. I like Chi Gong because it gives you a basic technique and you can build on it to make it yours. Like yoga, Chi Gong is a healing practice, never to be perfected, only improved upon.

If you can find a master in your area, that's wonderful, but it's not necessary. Two good home programs I like are Lee Holden and Ken Cohen. (www.leeholden.com & www.qigonghealing.com) Ken's is more traditional. Lee Holden is for everyone. Both are excellent. You can read about both online and decide which one to try. Don't stress over which is right, just try one and learn. Remember, it's about feeling and experiencing your body and how it moves. It's not about how much you can do in a short period. Relax.

Nutrition

Nutrition is essential to balance and healing. I don't believe in diets, but I do believe in listening to your body and eating what makes you feel healthy and energized. Fruits, veggies, nuts, complex carbs, protein are what work for most people. I won't elaborate on vegan, vegetarian, gluten-free, and so forth. If you want more information, my book *The Body Within Healing Challenge* breaks down the specific diets/lifestyles in more detail. Also, there is more information on my Body Within Community Website under resources. www.marieknoetig.com The point is, there's no one diet that's right for everyone. Pay attention to what you eat and how you feel after. If you are tired a half-hour after you eat, omit those foods and try different ones until you feel energized a half-hour after you eat. Pay attention--it pays off. The body never lies. You only fool yourself into thinking it is saying what you want.

Rest

Rest is extremely important. You should try to stick to a schedule, as much as possible, and you should never go to bed without taking some quiet time to stretch and do some relaxation breathing. If you go to bed stressed, you will sleep stressed. Your body does 90% of its healing during rest. If your body is stressed, how can it heal? Again, you can decide if this doesn't work for you, and that's okay. It's all about choice. One choice defines the next choice, and that's how you find clarity in your direction. Also, having a bedroom that has peaceful energy is important. Make sure the room is clutter free. The bed is not outdated and unsupported, keep electronics to a minimum and also make it smell good. Lavender oils are a great way to relax and aid in creating a restful sleep.

Finally, I tell my clients that they should have a hobby. Ideally, these are activities that quiet your mind and distract you from the hustle and bustle of everyday life. Just don't make a competition out of it, enjoy it and yourself while doing it. Perhaps try hiking, swimming, biking, reading, beading, crafts, fishing, and so forth. Be careful when choosing a hobby. I see so many people doing aggressive exercise and trying to keep up with others half their age and pushing their bodies to prove to themselves they can still do it. Not sure how that relaxes and destresses. Be careful. Chaos breeds chaos, balance breeds peace. If you don't have a hobby, keep looking and trying new things until you do. Your Body, Mind, and Spirit will love you for it.

Daily Check In

At night while doing your quiet time, check in to see how you are doing. Repeat daily check in to learn to balance ourselves and our lives around us so we can start to hear all the amazing messages, intuitively, just waiting for us. What do I consider balance and why is it so important? Balance is the power of three -Body, Mind, and Spirit. I believe we should balance all three. I believe they are all equal. Yes, I did say equal! So, if all three are equal, that means you should pay equal attention to your Body, Mind, and Spirit every day! Yes, every day! What that means is every day it's best if you check in with all three. Maybe twenty minutes at night before bed.

Your Body: How is your body doing? Does it need anything? Are you feeling tired? Maybe, some stretching? Was your nutrition sound today? Did you get any exercise today? Do you need exercise? Can you do better tomorrow?

Your Mind: Now you should think about your day. Check in to see if it was busy, manageable, and so forth. How did you handle issues that came your way? Did you see them clearly? Were you tired and unfocused? If you were how was your nutrition? Were you sharp and on task?

Next, *The Body Within* (your Spirit), did you hear it at all? Was it alerting you to anything? Did you listen or did you overrule it?

Just taking the time to self-evaluate daily connects you and rebalances you and opens the door for change. My challenge to you, as I give you the tools, is this: Try balancing all three and see if it has a positive effect on you and your daily living. See if it helps you discover triggers for your chronic pain or health issues. See if it alters you to why your kids are misbehaving. See if it helps you view yourself in a clearer light to know why your boss is always on your case. There are so many answers inside of us to all the nagging questions and problems that arise daily. Take the time with your Body Within and tap into the infinite possibilities we were all born with.

The Body Within

CHAPTER 10

It's All About Choices

I'M TAKING YOU BACK 18 years to a not-so-wise decision I made for myself after being in pain for many years. I chose to have a radical surgery to address Thoracic Outlet Syndrome.

Thoracic Outlet Syndrome occurs when nerves between the clavicle and first rib become pinched. It's very painful and, depending on the severity, can really impact the functioning of the arm. My doctors felt it was congenital, that I was born with it. However, eventually, I realized it had a lot to do with an accumulation of multiple injuries over time; specifically, my C-sections and the excessive scarring.

I had the surgery, and to put it mildly, my results were not good. I ended up with long thoracic nerve damage. I had a paralyzed serratus anterior muscle, which is the muscle that holds the scapula (part of the shoulder) to the body. The neurologist I was seeing told me it was a stretched nerve injury, and it would heal anywhere from one to three years.

Because of the previous injuries and the injury to the nerve in my shoulder, I had a lot of dysfunction in my upper torso and gait. My symptoms were severe headaches, chronic neck, shoulder, and back pain, and inability to hold posture, sit, or stand for any length of time.

Three years after the surgery, I was still trying to get back to a normal life, but the pain and desperation were almost constant. My primary care doctor sent me to a different neurologist, who did an EMG and informed me that there was no muscle--it never healed. Apparently, the nerve was severely damaged during the surgery. I guess I always knew because things weren't progressing as the doctors, physical therapists, and so forth said they would.

My primary care doctor was shocked and upset. He didn't know what to do with me, so he sent me to see a top neurologist at Mass General Hospital in Boston. Mind you, I decided to go to appease my PCP because, three years after surgery, I knew there really wasn't a lot that could be done.

After spending an hour with the Mass General doctor, he told me, much to my surprise, that he didn't think my symptoms were related to the surgery at all. Nor did he believe the nerve was scarred or damaged.

No, my doctor had another theory. He believed I had a degenerative muscular disease called Wilson's disease, and he proceeded to give me all the gory details. Wilson's disease is caused by the body's inability to rid itself of copper. The body has a natural ability to detox most metals and toxins, but with Wilson's disease, the body just does not know how. My doctor figured all of this out by examining me for an hour, and not reading any of my surgery, neurology, or physical therapy reports.

Naturally, my husband was devastated. I, on the other hand, was amused and told my doctor that he was way off base. "Look," I said to him, "three years ago, I went into the operating room with a different right arm than this one. I came out with a malfunctioning arm and right side of my body. I've been in this body for three years, watching some things become worse, and some things get better -- all while taking care of my three young children and going to school for my Exercise Science degree."

I went on to say that I knew I was getting stronger every day, but the shoulder muscles just would not cooperate. My doctor actually said to me, "You think you're getting better, but really you're in bad shape. Your body is not that of a 35-year-old woman. You have limited movement in how you walk and use your body. Your balance is off, and your right side is almost useless. How can you possibly think you are okay?" I smiled and said, "You should have seen me two years ago. I'm so much better and improving every day." He just smiled at me condescendingly.

Needless to say, my doctor and I had a heated discussion. He told me I needed to go for an MRI, a CT scan, blood work, and so forth and see an ophthalmologist to determine if I had what's called a "Kayser-Fleischer ring," around my cornea. That is the telltale sign of Wilson's disease. I declined all tests.

At that point, my doctor and my overwhelmed husband were tag teaming, but I kept saying, "I'm the one in this body. I may have the issues you say, but if I have Wilson's disease, I wouldn't be getting better." The doctor kept smiling and repeated with a chilly superiority, "You only think you're getting better." I spoke quietly and slowly to him as if to a child, "I've learned about body mechanics and myo- fascial twisting and I'm working on myself and my energy every day. I can see what the problems are. I just haven't been able to fix them completely yet. I am here for help, not a new diagnosis."

The shouting match ended with my doctor insisting, "This is very serious, and you're not listening to me." I responded teeth clenched, "You are not listening to me!" My husband, sitting there with a look of terror on his face, couldn't believe I was going toe to toe with this doctor. I knew he thought I should be listening to this man of science, not fighting him. In the end, I agreed to go to the ophthalmologist. But, I finished, "I'm not doing any other tests unless I have this Kayser-Fleisher ring in my eye." Both men relaxed and agreed, completely confident that they would be proven right.

Wilson's disease is rare. When I went to the ophthalmologist, I was in the exam room, and I could hear people in the hall talking about a "patient with a possible Kayser-Fleisher ring." I was practically in stitches because these medical professionals were waiting to witness this disease that I was certain I didn't have!

The eye doctor came in the room, I folded my arms. "I hate to burst your bubble and those of everyone waiting in the hall, but you're not going to find a Kayser-Fleisher ring." I told him the whole sordid tale to which he responded, "Well, your doctor is the best, so as much as you think you know, let us be the ones to decide what's going on with you." He then examined me, looked up, and put out his hand to shake mine. "Congratulations," he said. "You're right. You don't have Wilson's disease."

Now, can you imagine the upheaval my doctor at Mass General caused? For me? My husband? The eye doctors? Even for the other medical professionals huddling outside the door? All because my doctor had credentials and I didn't. He said "Jump," and all these people did. I said he was wrong, but I had no voice until the eye exam proved it. What is wrong with this picture? Why didn't I have a voice?

Do you have a voice when you are with doctors, surgeons, physical therapists, massage therapists, naturopaths, homeopaths, chiropractors, and so forth? When do you know enough to help yourself? It is essential that professionals acknowledge and respect what you already know about you.

The hardest part of my work is showing people how to heal themselves. Even when they do accomplish this feat, they don't believe that they did it themselves. They "blame" me (as I call it), or a supplement, or a drug they took. Some also credit divine intervention. They can't grasp that they could be their own answer. What has happened to us as a society that we don't have the confidence to know who we are and what we're truly capable of? Do we do it to ourselves with the choices we make, or has society done it to us by making us think we can't possibly know our own healing potential?

I challenge you to make a choice to try the exercises from the previous chapter and find one that feels right to focus on your energy. Wake up *The Body Within* and get to know it. Then add in stretching for 15-20 minutes before bed. Do it slow and pay attention to what is tight and what is not. Then focus on the tight areas to see if you can improve them. Get to know your body. If you can't stretch in certain areas use some oil and massage it. Get an anatomy book and see which direction the muscles go in and massage that way.

If you have had any injuries or have scars, massage, and rub out any bumps on the scars and make them soft. You will notice that helps when you are stretching—it makes it easier. You can even do it on your stomach.

If you choose to do the energy exercises, then stretch and massage tight areas before bed, you will relax and bring your focus on you – not the million things you have to get done. This will help you sleep better and help you heal while you are sleeping.

Next, I want you to really pay attention to what you eat and how it makes you feel. I also want you to learn about the nutritional value of what you eat. Make choices to change habits that are not serving you. This sounds like a lot but compared to the amount of time in a day that you don't feel sharp, energized, and balanced, it's really only minutes of your day. The last thing I would like you to do just before bed is to take a couple of cleansing breaths and ask *The Body Within* to show you what you need to see and ask to be open to seeing it. You probably won't see or sense anything at that moment but it will open you up so the next day as you are going about your daily routine, you may become aware to the things that you need to change or focus on.

This will help you to see the changes you need to make in order to create balance and healing.

What this will do for you is not only make you more aware of who you are, but you will know yourself better when you are faced with medical choices, and someone else is telling you how you feel. Doing these things will also empower you to know your body as you age so you can strengthen weaknesses as they occur not 20 years after they happen and then it's almost impossible.

Remember, do not ever give anyone the power to know you better than you know yourself. That is what healing is all about.

The Body Within

CHAPTER 11

Medicine

MY WORK IS COMPLEMENTARY to medicine. I work with whatever type of medicine my clients choose for their healing. I try not to take sides on one modality versus another, but I am human, so I do have personal preferences. Here, I would like to touch upon both Western philosophy and Alternative philosophy. There are many other types of medicine, but in my day-to-day job, I work with my clients to try to help them navigate a system of Western and Alternative medicine that are not always supportive of one another.

I really want you to understand that there is no right or wrong answer when choosing the type of medicine, you need. There's only lack of understanding about the roots of a particular medicine and how that form of medication derives its answers. I want you to see that you may distort how each one works for your own personal agenda rather than see the truth that lies behind both.

When using one modality or the other, you always need to be a major part of the healing process. The most important piece in any healing modality is just how critical a role <u>you</u> play in your own healing. I am not sure either Western medicine or Alternative addresses that properly. Look back 150 years ago at the meager tools we had available for healing in this country. How much did we have to help ourselves because of the limitations of medicine? If you didn't feel well, you <u>had</u> to rest. If you had an ailment, you sought advice from people you trusted. Then you had to help yourself get better because tools were so scant that the common cold could quite literally kill you.

Today, we either go to the doctor, pharmacy, or Alternative practitioner and get medications, supplements, and so forth. We read the label and take them accordingly. At what point do you even take a time out and ask your body what it needs? I bet most of us would hear the same answer. It might sound like, "Rest, less stress, better nutrition, more exercise, a better bed, shoes that are not broken down, support your spine, and so forth."

I find that people who favor Alternative medicine complain about the overuse of prescriptions, and those who side with Western medicine complain about the overuse of supplements. Alternative followers say, "Medicines can kill you, or damage the body. Plus, they only chase symptoms, they don't get rid of the cause."

Supporters of Western medicine fire back: Alternative uses too many supplements and herbs that just chase symptoms too. They can interfere with medicines, but they don't have to tell you. They are not FDA approved so we don't know what's really in them. Who's right?

What do you do if you want to try to use all the information out there, but you are overwhelmed? That's where getting to know *The Body Within* is crucial to help you intuitively to know when someone has an answer for you. Not the answer you want or even expect, but the answer you need.

Let's look at the Western medicine model and how it works. Western medicine is mainstream, evidence-based medicine. It's what most of us use our primary care doctors for. Then, if they can't help us, we see specialists in that particular field. This is what most insurance companies cover, and feel is acceptable medicine. It is evidence-based medicine. This means if 100 people break their arm, and they get put into a cast for six to eight weeks, 90 percent of patients will have the same or similar outcome. That's what makes for a proven treatment. Is it perfect for everyone? No. There's always   an   exception to the rule. If the first proven treatment doesn't work for you, you go to a specialist who brainstorms the problem and looks for additional proven treatments or drugs.

Are these treatments the only way to promote healing for an injury or illness? No, but they <u>are</u> tested treatments. Think about it. Any time your doctor writes a prescription and you go to the pharmacy to pick it up, you receive a pamphlet outlining how it can help you, and how it can hurt you. The drug has been tested in a lab -- repeatedly. It has also been tested on people for a specific period of time. This way you know what they're telling you has some validity. The testing and pharmaceutical companies back them up. Is it always 100% accurate? No, there are unforeseen problems with tested drugs; we regularly see this in the news.

That pamphlet you receive with your prescription details everything they've <u>seen</u> happen, but that doesn't mean other things can't. It's your choice to read the pamphlet, or not. It's your choice to use the drug or not. And, it's your choice to <u>listen</u> to your body when you're on the drug to see how it affects you.

Where does Alternative medicine get its treatments and how do they conclude that they work? First, you have to define Alternative medicine. Alternative medicine is a range of medical therapies that are not regarded as orthodox by the traditional/recognized medical profession. You can start with a naturopath, who has undergone eight years of schooling and training, to a homeopath, to an acupuncturist, to a chiropractor, to doctors and nurse practitioners who practice both Western and Alternative Medicine. Then, there are the people using computers to diagnose you with energy waves, or the practitioners who train in weekend seminars. Finally, there are the people who just say they're Alternative medicine practitioners with seemingly no substantial knowledge or training in any particular modality.

How do you safely navigate such a broad system? Remember Sam? He just thought if one treatment worked, they must all work.

Is Alternative medicine tested in a lab repeatedly to see if it creates a similar outcome? Again, based on my research, it really depends on who treats you. Naturopaths, chiropractors, and acupuncturists are becoming mainstream medicine and more accepted in the Western medicine circle because of their extensive training and their understanding of how to combine modalities. There is also more evidence to back up their modality. The problem is it's not the same kind of evidence documented the same way and available to the public on how they got their answer like the Western model. This is because the FDA does not regulate Alternative medicine, so they don't have to follow the same standards. Does that mean it does not work? No, it just means you have to trust your practitioner more because you have no way to research that what they are saying has a proven track record to yield those results.

Companies like Standard Process, Metagenics, and others spend a lot of money creating a lot of products and marketing them to chiropractors, doctors, nurse practitioners, and naturopaths. They teach these practitioners how they're tested, how to use them, and why they work. They don't follow FDA guidelines because they are not prescription drugs. But are these supplements used to treat and diagnose illness, even though they claiming they do not? Are they tested against the drugs from pharmaceutical companies? The answer to those questions is why there is a huge obstacle in merging the two modalities.

Supplement companies are not required to follow the same guidelines as pharmaceutical companies, so it's hard to know what to use in conjunction with treatments you're already undergoing. While I find many supplements to be useful, being a critical thinker, I would like to see a label on them just like pharmaceuticals. I'd want to know the risks, benefits, and possible drug interactions, or contraindications so that we know how they combine with other medications and supplements safely. This omission is why most doctors simply say, "Don't use it." They cannot prove it's safe and effective. For me, what I struggle with is, I treat many clients taking a lot of supplements and there is a universal belief in the Alternative world among users is it's all natural so it cannot harm you. When they need surgery, they are asked to stop taking their supplements ten days before in case there may be interactions. Most clients think nothing can happen to them. I go through their list, and some are natural blood thinners, stimulants, blood pressure regulators, and so forth. If they can alter the working of your body, then there is the possibility of harm whether it is natural or not. Please understand that.

When I talk about the need for labels on supplements, all I read or hear is, "It costs too much money." Yet, the last article I read about the latest Cystic Fibrosis drug said it took one billion dollars - from start to finish – to get it to market. The pharmaceutical company had to pay that. If I were a supplement company, I would avoid that expense at all costs too.

However, therein lies the problem. Failing to hold supplement companies to the same standard as drug companies is preventing a genuine collaboration. Worse, it leaves a giant gap in the system for all of us trying to make informed choices.

My personal opinion is that specific supplements that are prescribed by doctors or Alternative practitioners as medical treatments
– in particular, for cancer - should be tested the same way pharmaceuticals are tested for cancer treatments. They should also be tested alongside the already approved drugs and treatment protocols available for cancer patients now. That way, patients are able to get the same type of information so they can make health care choices on a level field. I have so many cancer patients who want to take products such as probiotics, or green drinks and cancer-specific supplements to boost their immune systems during treatment. Doctors and treatment facilities tell them not to, concerned that these products will diminish the effect of treatment. They don't know if they will; they just can't say if they will or won't. Meanwhile, the alternative practitioner says, "Take it. It won't interfere with chemo." How do they know that, and the other guy doesn't? Again, who is right? Another big concern I have with how cancer is treated Alternatively is the trail of evidence. I have many clients come to me who have exhausted all their time, energy, finances, and internal power trying to navigate a system that has no foundation, as I refer to it. If I receive a cancer diagnosis and choose the Western model for treatment, my

primary care physician helps me to get to an oncologist. Then the oncologist sets up treatments and if I don't agree, my primary care physician will help me find another opinion. There are also many facilities all over the country to help you with second opinions. Then you can find out more information to support what treatment is recommended by doctors, friends, or even the internet. If you have insurance, most consults and treatments are covered.

My experience with clients using the Alternative model has been this – once you choose Alternative medicine, the primary care physician very rarely supports you. You have to find the practitioner or treatment center via word of mouth or internet search. There is no insurance coverage for your blood work or treatments, so you are already in it for thousands of dollars. Then the supplements, IV's, and so forth are all out-of-pocket, and sometimes most of your friends think you aren't treating your cancer and they may even think you're being stupid. Sometimes the family supports the patient, sometimes not. It's very hard to find information online to back up this evidence. The second opinions are even harder because the next practitioner's treatment is completely different and costly with no way to research it. That is why tapping into *The Body Within* and living in balance is so important to help you navigate an overwhelming system. It is also why progressive integrative medicine is vital, as well as places that mimic the Cancer Treatment Center of America model. It's lonely to have cancer, but it's even lonelier if you choose to use the Alternative route.

You owe it to yourself to be informed consumers when using either Western medicine or Alternative medicine; I find the patient is usually misled into believing what the practitioner believes, not necessarily what the facts say. As I've said throughout this book, do your homework. Again, ask yourself: How well do I know this person treating me? Research your options, then work on balancing yourself and listen to *The Body Within*.

One of the most prevalent misunderstandings I see in patients is when a new drug, supplement, or procedure comes out. Patients just assume every practitioner must be doing it or using it. They figure they don't have to do their own research because they think they'll automatically get the latest advances in medicine. Or sometimes, the patient wants the new drug on the market, even though the old one has a better history. So, they force the hand of the practitioner to think their way.

Here's a perfect example. One of my clients decided to have a hip replacement. Betty, middle-aged, tall, thin, very intelligent did her due diligence, researched one procedure from the other and made an educated medical decision for herself. Betty chose a surgeon who practiced the newest procedure – he performed the surgery from the front of the hip. The rehabilitation with this approach is very short; you're up and around the same day or the next. Betty's outcome was positive.

When Betty's dad heard how well the surgery went for her, he decided to have the much-needed procedure. But Arthur lives in another state. He came out of surgery with less favorable results than Betty and a lot more rehabilitation. Why? Because Arthur's surgeon doesn't perform the new and improved surgery that Betty's surgeon did on her. Arthur's surgeon still does the standard side incision surgery. You can imagine how stunned Betty and Arthur were to learn that the medical field still offers this older, less progressive procedure.

Arthur's two mistakes? First, he never asked his daughter exactly what type of hip replacement surgery she had. Second, he didn't ask his surgeon for any details about how he approached the surgery and when the doctor explained he just assumed that was what his daughter had done. Guess what? You get what your physician believes is right or what level of education the practitioner has progressed to or what the hospital he or she works for allows. That's not always what you want.

Here's another example. Many of my female clients have talked about using thermography for breast cancer detection. I was puzzled at first. They told me that thermos-scans are a substitute for mammograms, and they're told it's better at detection and a lot safer and more accurate than a mammogram. However, the company website actually states that a thermos-scan should be used alongside a mammogram for the best possible outcome for detection and diagnosis, not replace it. Again, are you getting what the practitioner believes or what the science shows?

One of my favorite ways to learn more about navigating the overwhelming medical system is to listen to Doctor Radio. It's a radio show on the Sirius network. The show is based out of the NYU Langone Medical Center. There is a different modality on every hour or so, and their top doctors DJ the programs. They have a wide variety of guest speakers, from scientists to supportive medicine practitioners and individuals that write books on how to heal. They allow the audience, that would be you, to call in with your own questions about medical conditions, second opinions, or just your own advice to them. They help you understand drug therapies, the latest research, and the new and available treatments. My favorite part is how human the doctors are. Some of the DJs disagree with the guest's theories, some DJs agree or are learning something new just like the listener. Some of the shows tend to be very conservative about mixing Alternative medicine with Western medicine. Then with some of the shows like sports medicine and dermatology, you get a much broader view. Do yourself a favor and check it out. I honestly believe it saves lives because of the information given, how it's delivered, and how they make you part of the learning. It's a great tool to help you make more informed decisions.

How are you making healthcare decisions? Are they based on fear, lack of research, or trusting in someone else's interpretation of the science? It's all about being in touch with your intuition, *The Body Within*, so when you are making medical decisions, you are balanced enough to see the information clearly, not the way your emotions or others interpret it.

I met a woman recently who was a breast cancer survivor. Lovely, delicate-looking, nature-loving Martha chose a mastectomy instead of a lumpectomy to avoid chemo or radiation. She also chose to have her ovaries removed to avoid taking hormone suppressors for the rest of her life. Martha did her research and decided these one-time surgeries would prevent drug damage, over time, to her body. She also knew the surgeries would rid her of cancer.

However, Martha then went on to tell me that she felt like maybe she had made her decision based on fear. "Maybe I should have tried to heal alternatively," I asked Martha why she didn't choose Alternative at the time. Her answer? "My gut told me that I wouldn't be able to make the necessary changes. I didn't feel I was disciplined enough to devote the time and resources to alternative healing, I was not sure I knew a reason why I had cancer, so how could I heal it? I just didn't feel it was my answer."

How then, I asked her, could her decision have been fear-based if she saw it clearly, from all sides, and knew herself completely? She explained that she has always lived a very organic lifestyle and since her cancer treatment, she had talked to her circle of peers and read articles about healing Alternatively. They made her feel like she failed by not choosing that route. Let's recap. Martha did the research, questioned all sides, and knew her own truth. She then made a decision that gave her the best possible outcome. If that's failure, I would hate to see success. What I took from my conversation with Martha is that society doesn't reward us for bold, informed choices, so how can we really have confidence in ourselves to make them? So many questions, so little time.

Understand this: by the time you develop cancer, your body is tired. Furthermore, there's no true understanding of how you created it -- or you wouldn't have cancer in the first place. How long do you think it takes to learn the true depth of who you are? To realize that your genetics, family history, lifestyle, environment, and choices you've made in life have brought you to this defining moment?

If you know your truth, healing will prevail whether you choose an Alternative or a Western mode. Just don't think for a second that just the medicine is the real answer. The real answer, my friend, is you.

Medicine, whether it's conventional or Alternative, has flaws. So, it's up to you to understand what your health issues are, to do your research, and when you decide on treatment, determine the long-term and short-term effects of it. If any practitioner tells you that they have your answer, and there are no side effects to a particular treatment, consider those red flags. Run fast and hard to find a new practitioner. Any time you add medicine and/or supplements or alter the natural working of the human body, there is an effect. It's your choice whether you want to accept the degree of change to your body or not.

You can create your own reality (how you perceive the world around you and how you want it to be) to make life what you want it to be. You can't create reality, (what is really happening in the world around you) reality just is. With that said, repeat after me:

> I am quieting my mind, embracing my soul. I
> am open to all possibilities in my healing.

CHAPTER 12

Choosing Your Truth

AS I PEERED AROUND the corner and looked into the room, the hospital bed was at a slight incline, and her hands were in prayer position. Wrapped in them was the rosary she's had since the beginning of her Convent days. In so many ways, all the years spent devoted to God were very fulfilling for Carol. However, in other ways, Carol was a conflicted woman -- conflicted because she never fully understood why she had chosen this path for her life.

When Carol was a young woman if you wanted more than to become a wife and a mother you had few options, namely nurse, teacher, secretary, or nun. Financially, Carol's family was not able to help her pursue higher education, so she made the logical choice. Carol became a nun and devoted her life to the Catholic Church. At first, her commitment to God sustained her.

However, as time went on, and the teachings changed, Carol started to see how the Church was changing. She struggled with watching the personal agendas of those in charge take priority over the faith. Carol's own faith was often shaken over the years, and she sometimes had doubts about her calling. But after devoting so much of her life to being a nun – a servant of God – what else could she be? Who else could she be?

The years passed, and eventually, Carol's fear of the unknown became greater than any doubts or questions she had about the religion or the Church. She chose to shelter herself in what she knew to be safe.

Now, lying in bed, surrounded by her closest sisters, companions, and the little family she has left, Carol seems to be at peace, knowing that the selfless life she's led, devoted to God, and the welfare of others will guarantee her safe passage to Heaven. Though she is secure that she will go to Heaven, she does not realize that she must let go of this life to move on to the next.

As the minute's tick by, everyone waits and prays, prays, and waits, and then, it happens. Carol's cancer-stricken body can no longer sustain life, and she dies. Everyone in the room is saddened but also relieved - and confident - that Carol is with God now, her Father. After all, could there possibly be any other outcome?

Yes, there was. As I recount this story for you, Carol is still – as we say – Earthbound. She is choosing to <u>not</u> move forward because the forward is not what she expected. All her life she has given away her internal power. She has never truly tapped into *The Body Within* and had a true conversation with herself. She chose a life of others defining how she should think, act, and respond, how she should live. Am I saying if you become a nun, you don't go to Heaven? Absolutely not. The question I'm posing is: When Carol chose this path for her life, did she do so because she felt it was her truth? Or was it the truth she <u>thought</u> she had to live?

Many times, over the years, Carol questioned if being a nun was the right life for her. But she never allowed herself to make it about her, and what she genuinely wanted or believed. Instead, she allowed society, and what she was taught, to decide for her. Carol lived a life devoted to God, but was she living her truth?

Healing comes from being in touch with your soul – *The Body Within* and understanding who you are and what you need to heal. Healing is about living your truth, not someone else's. If Carol never questioned whether or not she was living her truth, then how could she know who she was at a soul level? How could she be in touch with herself in order to free herself?

Carol's ending was surreal. Cancer, the seizures, the inability to care for herself, the pain and suffering. She wondered the entire time If I've done everything right then, why? I'm so young; I'm only in my 50s. Why?

Carol and I have had many conversations since her death, and she is still in a state of dismay. All she has to do is move forward, but her reluctance to do so is reminiscent of how she lived her life. The safety and security of what she knows right now is easier than taking a leap of faith and trusting that what's ahead is that amazing place she hoped for. It's just not the way she thought it would be.

Many times, her gut spoke to her. She struggled with what she believed to be the truth, and she struggled with what might be her truth. If you look at how things turned out for her, was there peace in who she was, or constant unease in her gut? If she had questioned her path, she would have had to make some choices that might have diverted her from her chosen path. Then again, such a seeking may have led her right back to being a nun, this time with a doubt-free, absolute knowing that is who she truly was.

To be clear, Carol is not earthbound because she chose to be a nun. Carol is earthbound because she allowed family, fear, society, and the Church to decide her truth for her. In time, Carol will see that it is an infinite God and an infinite Universe, and no one has the absolute truth. That she has always been, and will always be, in control of her destiny. Is she stuck in limbo? Define stuck. She is where she is by choice or stubbornness. You can call that stuck. She wants what she believed to be true, not what is. How is that different than any one of us?

If you are someone struggling with chronic pain or illness, sit quietly and do you mini-me exercises from Chapter 6. Ask to see what you need to see about what is draining your healing energy. Then, let it go. For the next day, see if you become aware of behaviors or choices that are throwing you out of balance. It does not have to be as big as a career choice like Carol. It could be your present job, your relationships, how you view yourself, others, your nutrition, and rest. Remember, chaos breeds chaos and balance breeds peace. Many little realizations add up to a lot of healing in the bigger picture.

Take a walk on the wild side and get to know *The Body Within* to determine where your healing comes from.

CHAPTER 13

Learning to Listen

My mom passed away from breast cancer, and I thought I would share a little bit about her passing with you. When I tell people my mom had breast cancer, they expect a story about a long battle and a tough fight. My mom had fought for 31 days before she lost her battle with breast cancer. When we found out she had cancer, it took them several days to pinpoint it to breast cancer. She fought as hard as she could to beat this horrible illness but unfortunately, the cancer had spread through her body, and she lost her fight 31 short days after entering the hospital for some routine "tests."

The reason I'm telling this story is if she had gone to the doctor for her annual checkup, she would most likely be here. Her grandchildren would know her laugh, her smile, and the warmth of her hug. She would've been here for the many milestone events that have happened in the last six years since she passed. Yes, she is here in spirit and watching over us, we know, but it's not the same. I'm posting this because everyone deserves a chance to fight, my mom didn't get one. Early detection is SO important; it really is a fighting chance.

- Kathleen White

WHAT IS INTUITION OR listening to *The Body Within*, and how can you use it every day to better your life, so you do not end up in the same boat as Sam (Ch.6), Mary (Ch. 5), and Sister Carol (Ch.12), and have more control of your life, your health, and your healing?

What does intuition have to do with helping you heal chronic pain or illness, help you live a long healthy life, and eventually die peacefully? Better yet, how can intuition help you avoid getting sick in the first place? Let's start by looking at how often you ignore your intuition instead of embracing its power. On the following pages, I introduce you to a few people who either discarded or embraced their intuition and how living in a pattern of choosing one way or another influenced their journey. When it comes to intuition, you always have a choice: Listen or ignore.

My neighbor, Joe, of 20+ years, was about 62 and had just retired. His wife told me that Joe passed out and ended up in the hospital. Many tests later, he found out he had colon cancer. Emergency surgery was performed to remove a large section of his intestines, and it was determined that the cancer had spread to his lymph nodes. Joe was very upset and very surprised. He couldn't believe this happened to him.

Really? He was a smoker, drinker, had never exercised, or cared much about his diet. For all the years I knew Joe, he told me regularly, "You never know what can happen to you. You could retire and die right away. So, I am going to retire as young as I can." At what point, in the five years before passing out, did Joe not notice stomach discomfort, weakness, flu-like symptoms and most of all, his intuition telling him something was wrong? I must have heard the story about how he was going to retire young 200 times since we had met. Didn't Joe hear his gut telling him to get himself checked? Furthermore, why didn't Joe go for his regular checkups? He was of diagnostic age to have a colonoscopy. He had a good job and good insurance. If Joe had done all these things and listened to the inner voice telling him he might not enjoy his retirement, would he have done the preventative care? Would it have made a difference? Unfortunately, Joe died shortly after his retirement, as he predicted.

Then there is my Aunt Lynn, who lived in California her whole life. A wonderful woman devoted to her family. She collapsed, went to the hospital, and was diagnosed with Stage 4 breast cancer. She died about a month later. Like Joe, Lynn didn't go for regular exams or mammograms. Leading up to the day she collapsed, weren't there times when she just didn't feel well? Why couldn't her intuition get through to alert her that all was not well? She was a very intuitive person with her kids, her husband, and her job. Why not herself? If she had been intuitive with herself, would that have made a difference? Her daughter, Kathleen feels it would have made a difference. Kathleen, her youngest daughter, posted the introduction to this chapter on her Facebook page in hopes it would make a difference for someone else's family. I hope it does as well.

Intuition is as simple as feeling the need to double check that you have your car keys, even though you typically don't forget them. It's feeling something is not quite right with a loved one. Most importantly, it's paying attention to the health signs coming from your own body. (This is why it is very important to be balanced and know yourself.) Listening to intuition gives you answers in all areas of your life – health, wealth, jobs, relationships, and your children. It helps you make better decisions for yourself and others. It could be little things like your intuition telling you to slow down. Stop taking on other people's drama. Relax more. Exercise. Eat better. Any of these sound familiar? Could actually paying attention to these intuitive messages be your answer to preventing your health crises, saving your marriage, getting along with your kids, or even avoiding adversity in your life?

Our bodies are amazing healers all by themselves. If you cut yourself, your body stops the bleeding by clotting. If I cut off your arm, your body will immediately slow the blood flow to the arm, so you don't bleed as quickly. How does it know how to do that, yet you don't think the body can heal other ailments and illnesses?

Intuition: (def.) a natural ability or power that makes it possible to know something without any proof or evidence; a feeling that guides a person to act a certain way without fully understanding why

Everyday life is filled with moments to act on intuition. You get up in the morning, start to grab a donut, and something inside says, that's going to make me feel like crap. Plus, I don't need the calories. Maybe, I should take the time to eat something healthier. At that moment, you make a decision for better or worse. You start your day with a gut feeling. Did you ignore it or act on it? If you had acted on it, would it have made a difference in your day?

You go to work. Your co-worker, Sally, doesn't seem like herself today. Something is off. You ask if she's okay, and Sally says she's fine. Your intuition tells you differently, but you choose to ignore it rather than press Sally further. An hour later, all hell breaks loose because Sally was in a really bad place and snapped. What if you had just taken that extra second to say "Sally, are you sure you're okay? I have time. Let's get some coffee and just talk."

Every minute of every day is filled with these gut feelings. The most successful people in life learned early on to follow this intuition rather than get caught up in everyone else's opinions. One rather unfortunate problem is most of these people only listen to intuition in one area of their life and feel it has no place elsewhere. I've seen very successful professionals – many of them clients – build impressive empires. They put enormous time, energy, and focus into their business with flawless intuition. Unbelievably, these same people have zero intuition when it comes to their health or family issues. It's not because it doesn't exist, it's just that they have tunnel vision.

I heard a statistic recently: 150,000 people die every year from drug reactions. What if you had a bad feeling that the doctor gave you the wrong prescription or this medicine was going to cause you harm and you researched it? What would the outcome be? That would be an interesting study. How many people have had that happen to them? I know many people, including myself, who have caught a doctor's error. It doesn't mean you lose confidence in him or her or have to find a new physician. It just means, 1) you see medicine as a tool with strengths and weaknesses 2) your doctor is human, and 3) ultimately, you're the one in charge of your own healthcare.

Let's reflect on Mary's case again from chapter 5. Wasn't there a point at which Suzanne's gut told her that the doctors were wrong? Of course, there was. So why did she continue to go back time and time again? Didn't she know her own truth, that she might actually know her daughter better than the doctor? But does society, and our medical system, allow mothers and other caregivers to know more? And if Suzanne pushed harder, how much confidence, time, and energy to stay the course with her concerns? Then, does she prevail?

And Mary's intuition told her that the headaches might be coming from her shoulders, but she didn't think for a second that her opinion had any value. Not with her doctor. Not with her mother. Why didn't the doctor or Suzanne sense that Mary had input but was holding back? Again, does society and our current medical model teach that a teenager like Mary could possibly know her own body?

Maybe in science class, at a young age, it's my opinion, we should be educating our children on not only the anatomy of the body but how the body works and our role in being one with it. Learning how much power you have to keep it safe and healthy and how you should listen to how you feel every day according to what you eat, how much you move, sleep, or exercise.

I worked with a 17-year-old athlete who had scoliosis and a lot of myofascial twisting. Kevin, an excellent basketball player, who was always actively volunteering to help others had high pain levels and was looking for answers. We started working together, along with physical therapy, and he was getting excellent results. Kevin had to take a break from our sessions to go on a trip, and when he came back, it was time for a follow-up with his doctor. His doctor felt that physical therapy had not corrected enough of the problem, and Kevin's body had done as much healing as it could. Really? At seventeen, the body is finished healing in his doctor's opinion, the only option left was to put Kevin in a back brace.

Kevin couldn't believe what he was hearing. Not because his doctor suggested a brace, but because Kevin knew, in his gut, that he was healing and changing every day. He knew his body was moving better. He wasn't in as much pain, and he could reach and stretch in ways he hadn't been able to in some time. But his doctor was only using one guide to assess improvement, and he convinced Kevin's mother, Corinne, that a brace was the medically appropriate next step. Kevin was adamant. In order for his body to heal, he needed full mobility and to continue challenging the muscles that hadn't functioned well. Kevin's intuition was screaming, my doctor and my mother are wrong. The brace is only going to make matters worse! They thought Kevin was just a kid who didn't understand the magnitude of his decision.

Let's look at this objectively: Kevin is 17, an athlete, and a straight A student going off to college. But he doesn't get a say in his own healthcare? Kevin's gut was on fire, telling him that the doctor was wrong. If his mother and his doctor are wrong, what can he do or say? Next time his gut speaks loudly, will Kevin listen? Fortunately, Kevin had a lot of moxie, and his doctor and his mother did what he wanted. Kevin continued healing, and today he is at a good place, inside and out. He achieved healing no one thought possible. He was a very open young man, intuitive, and knew what was best for his health.

So, again, the question: who was right? Was it his doctor and his mother because they are older and more experienced? Or was it Kevin, who was getting clear information from his gut that he was right? In this case, everyone was right. The doctor and Corinne made decisions based on the knowledge and information available to them within the parameters of medicine. Kevin used the information at his disposal as well – his intuition and everything he had learned from our work together and all the things he could do to help himself. But here's the disconnect: Kevin's intuition – the knowing coming from his gut – was not a proven medical treatment, so how could he possibly be right? Yet, look at his pain levels. They had decreased significantly. His spine was getting stronger, his range of motion was increasing, and he was finally able to return to his active lifestyle. Still, Corinne operating in fear mode, and the doctor, following medical protocol, decided that Kevin couldn't be accurate in his own self-assessment. Hence, Kevin wasn't heard until he pushed hard enough and they finally listened.

Kevin was able to see reality clearer than most adults. His parents have done an incredible job raising him. Now they need to realize the need to heal themselves. As Kevin gets stronger in self, his parents, who wanted him to see life clearly, now have to adjust to him being able to live on his own in a lot of ways.

One of my favorite TV shows is NCIS. If you've seen it, you know that the main character, Agent Gibbs, always gets his man even when the clues or evidence say otherwise. His gut tells him differently, and he keeps digging until he finds the truth. It's a fun way to see how he pushes the people around him to trust his gut above the evidence.

So, here's my challenge: Take a walk on the wild side and go with your gut, even if it doesn't make sense. You may be right, or you may be wrong. Even when you're wrong, it teaches you more about what you believed to be right.

Take the time to learn about yourself and where your health is at this time. Do you have a chronic illness, pain, aging, and so forth? Know yourself, then sit quietly and ask to see what you need to see about your health. Then wait. It may take time, but as you are going through your day and your mind is distracted, you might get awareness of how you can help yourself or how you see things differently.

Those are moments to embrace and reflect upon. They will show you how you give away your healing power and that you have much more tools than you even thought. Healing not only comes from medicine--it comes from you seeing what's depleting your healing energy and throwing you out of balance.

Give it a try. You never know what you might learn about yourself.

The Body Within

CHAPTER 14

Passing Peacefully

THERE I WAS, SITTING in the neonatal intensive care unit of the Dartmouth-Hitchcock Hospital with my three-day-old grandson, Zack, who had undergone life-saving surgery. His little, eight-pound body was sleeping peacefully. The room was small, with just six cribs in the section we occupied. The crib next to Zack's was no more than eight feet away. Fortunately, we were mostly by ourselves except for the set of triplets nearby. It was impossible not to notice or overhear conversations as we were practically sitting on top of each other. It was apparent that one of the babies was very ill and the doctors didn't feel he would survive.

The parents and grandparents were clustered around the babies, trying to process the possibility of losing one. I overheard them talking about the weak one. "I hope he can hold his own until the priest gets here," I heard them say. "He has to hold on." At that moment, I knew he was dying, and they were hoping to get him baptized quickly, so his little soul would be protected and go to Heaven.

A short time later, the nurse said they were moving us to another area for a couple of hours so the baptism could take place. As we cleared out of the area, I glanced toward the sick baby as I had been doing for a couple of days. This time, I saw the baby's energy detached from his body, waiting outside the crib, waiting to die. I was puzzled. Why was the baby's energy outside his body, not with it? Why not just die? Then, I remembered what the parents kept saying: I hope he can hold on until the priest gets here.

Then I realized: The baby was reading his parents' intent. An hour later, we came back and learned that the baby had died just minutes after the baptism. My guess is that the parents' intent changed. They relaxed as soon as he was baptized, and the baby felt the freedom to let go. Would you consider this a peaceful dying? As soon as the baby was baptized, he died. Did he/she do it on their own or was the passing influenced by others' thoughts and beliefs? The point of this sweet story is to show that we do affect others—how we treat them, how they prepare to live, how they prepare to die and everything in between.

Do your thoughts and beliefs affect others in your life, of all ages, trying to die? Trying to heal? Trying to learn a new way to help themselves? The biggest complaint I hear from a lot of my chronically ill or chronic pain clients is a lack of community in their healing journey. It's as simple as they might have a food allergy or many food allergies and their family and friends instead of helping them, they undermine them by making comments like, "how can you go without eating that?" "I would never eat that!" "How can you eat that? It looks terrible!" Your world becomes smaller; events are less enjoyable, and you feel more detached when you have to make two of everything to satisfy everyone at dinner.

How does this baby's death story connect into the living?

Let's take another look at my mother-in-law as an example of how we all should aspire to live, and then end this journey. Was Grace blinded by others' thoughts and beliefs in the room? No. Did she have an opinion that one way was better than another? Or was she living her truth of what she understood life to be? Yes. She was open to all possibilities in her healing, as was I. She took a leap of faith in that hospital room and hoped I would trust what was happening and just let it all unfold. For my part, I felt the energy pull and had no idea what would happen, but my gut said, go with it, and you'll see. Now, had I had an opinion; I would have shut the whole thing down.   Unfortunately, my simple mind would not have been able to see that any of that was even possible. Neither of us decided based on what we thought could happen, or feared could happen, we just allowed it to happen. That, my friends, is the hardest part to process and the hardest way to live. We fight our deficiencies instead of embracing what is. If you learn more now about where true healing comes from, it will all transfer to all facets of your life because dying is no different than living. You just have an emotional block that makes you perceive it differently.

As an energy practitioner, I foster my intuition many hours a day. This is a big part of why I can feel and understand what most of my clients need. There are always events leading up to you healing yourself, but if you can't see the choices or openings coming your way, you may take the right turn instead of the left. In lieu of an amazing outcome, you end up with the only outcome possible as a result of the choices you made along the way. My goal is to teach you to slow down, to see the opening, and to let the miracles happen.

I have read stories written about primitive tribes who know when it's time to die. They give their belongings away, say goodbye, lay down, and let go. They die a peaceful, conscious death. Are those stories true? Can that really happen? What about people being diagnosed with terminal cancer and they choose not to treat it and then the cancer is gone? Why can't you do any of these things? Or can you? Why do you fight death and have no concept of what it means to let go? Do you even know you're fighting it? Why do you fight believing that you have the ability to heal yourself from illness and disease? I have a client, Bill, whose mom Sophia was in her 90s, and she just wanted to die. He told me all the time, "She should just let go." He didn't know why she wouldn't.

So, I challenged him. "If I told you to die right now, how would you let go?" He got frustrated with me., "I don't know, you just let go!" He thought it was easier than it really was, even though he didn't know how himself. After countless conversations with Bill explaining that his mother had no idea how to die. She was fearful and many other beliefs throughout her life, including that she didn't understand the true power she had inside to know and heal herself. It was what kept her here; I think the bell finally went off in his head. I could see he finally understood that she did not know that she was in control.

Bill brought his mom home from the nursing home for a holiday dinner with his family. On the ride to his home, she opened up the conversation once more about how she was tired and just wanted to die. This time, instead of Bill ignoring the comment as he usually did, he took a walk on the wild side. With a quiet voice, he asked, "What do you think will happen? Are you afraid?" They ended up having a nice chat, and Bill was able to comfort her. "It might not be what you think. Maybe you can just relax and let go." This seemed to allay some of her fears. They both saw a new way of looking at an old problem.

Sophia had a nice dinner with her family, and when Bill was driving her back to the nursing home, she died in the car. Although it was outside his comfort zone, Bill had relaxed with her and guided by helping her make the transition to the next step of her journey. I was so happy for his mom, but most of all, for Bill. He opened a new window for more possibilities inside himself. Now, he sees himself differently, puts more time and energy into learning about himself and healing the ailments he felt he had no power to address. He really began to feel like he was more. (He woke up *The Body Within*.) All it takes is a split second of awareness to create a new path for our lives to take. So, if what you're doing isn't working, give some air to a new thought. Miracles can happen if you make space for them.

When I do energy work with my clients, I teach them how to lay hands on themselves and clean their energy, just like this book shows you. When I lay hands, they can usually feel the energy moving. Sometimes, they feel the tissue healing and the body realigning as I hold space, sometimes not. When my clients do feel it for the first time, it makes them uncomfortable ("What is it I'm feeling?"), but in time, they find a sense of peace and realize it's all them. My intent with clients is always to help them help themselves. Some clients embrace the practice, learn, and really make changes toward healing.

Others feel uncomfortable if I'm not the one facilitating. Some clients really work to master their skills and heal themselves. Other clients try too hard and want a step-by-step guide to relaxing and feel their own energy. But there is no one-size-fits-all How-to Handbook. It's about learning who you are, and what works for you. It's following *The Body Within.*

As you do the exercises and learn to feel your energy, realize that <u>this</u> is the energy of your soul or *The Body Within.* When you tap into *The Body Within*, you're able to connect and be guided in your own healing. Don't judge it, don't even have an opinion. Just be with it and see what happens.

The biggest disconnect in most healing modalities is not recognizing and not understanding how much ability you have to help yourself and that dying is as healing to one as is living. I just want people to use all the knowledge available to them, whether it is Western medicine or Alternative to help you with this topic. You just need to know what knowledge is truly right for you.

Further, your body is your temple, not your dumpster. As you learn that you have an energetic being, your soul - *The Body Within*, that's when true transformation starts to happen. As you become more aware of *The Body Within*, you start to understand its needs and how you can affect your quality of life.

As you start to feel your energy, you'll be drawn to such practices such as energy clearing or laying hands on body parts or sitting quietly. Let your intuition guide you. Only you know what you're feeling and how you're being guided to help yourself. The more you practice, the stronger your guidance becomes. The more you listen to *The Body Within*, the more your life comes back into balance.

As you become more balanced, you start to realize what your body needs as far as rest, relaxation, nutrition, exercise, stimulation for the brain, human interaction, and so forth. Only then, will you really start to feel alive?

As you grow into who you truly are, at a soul level, you become one with your path or truth. All your choices become conscious, including how you live and how you die. You'll be guided because you know how and what you feel. If you've never tapped into your soul, how will you ever know what it feels like? If you don't know what it feels like, how will it guide you to what you need now for everyday health and wellness all the way until you pass of old age?

As a society, we're so good at keeping ourselves alive because we fear death so much. Hence, how could you possibly know when it's time to let go or how to do it? Do you truly think those suffering in nursing homes really want to be there, or do they simply know no other way? Can you change that destiny for them? I believe for some, yes, for some, no. Can you change it for yourself? I believe, yes.

Over time, I have seen stories like Grace's become less rare. It all goes back to being open and hearing the messages coming from outside your aura. The more muck in your energy, the harder it is to see the answers you need to correct your health issues now and to help you age gracefully even when they're right in front of you.

As we wrap up this chapter, I urge you to practice the energy tools from Chapter 6. If you start to feel your energy flowing, keep working at it. If you have a question, visit my website The Body Within Healing Community at http://www.bodywithinhealing.net/ for many self-help tips from my years of experience and also what others have shared. Hopefully, it will help you in your journey. The stronger you sense energy, the easier it is to clear out your muck, and the more your intuition grows.

This will benefit you in all aspects of your life - health, wealth, family, relationships. And, yes, even when it's time to die. I wish you happy healing and a stronger connection to you.

CHAPTER 15

Childbirth

Natural Childbirth

Childbirth involving little or no use of drugs or anesthesia and usually involving a program in which the mother is psychologically and physically prepared for the birth process.

MY NIECE JENNA, WHOM I love dearly, was 8 ½ months pregnant. In her tall, thin body she looked about four months pregnant and was carrying the baby very high. Her partner came to me, worried that she might have a problem delivering. He felt it at a gut level and didn't know why. "I've always known things," he said to me, "and this is one of those times I feel something is not right."

I already had the same feeling, so I agreed to try and help Jenna figure out where this energy was coming from. At this point, I had been uninvolved because Jenna's vision of childbirth was different to mine and as much as I am a caring Aunt, I was supporting her in her vision but now there was more information. Jenna has a physical illness that's resulted in numerous surgeries on her throat and larynx. All of these surgeries and resulting scar tissue have caused a lot of myofascial twisting in her body. I suspected that the baby was caught in some of the twisting under her ribs and hadn't dropped to create a smooth delivery. This can happen when the natural movement of the body has been disrupted by outside forces (like her multiple surgeries) and myofascial twisting of the tissue in her torso.

I approached Jenna. "How do you feel about delivering the baby?" She sighed. "I'm very anxious but was afraid to share my feelings. Something's not right." Her facial expression was very worried. "I had a dream that I was delivering the baby and I couldn't breathe. The baby just wouldn't come out." Also knowing all the breathing issues, she has had in life only seemed to bring more anxiety.

Jenna said she had tried to talk to her OB about it, but this OB discounted her concerns as "new mom worry." I wish I could say this kind of response was an anomaly, but I'm afraid it's not. Sometimes, your intuition is very strong, but there is no scientific evidence to back up what you are feeling so how can they believe you? Sometimes, some people just worry too much so how are they supposed to know which is which? (That is where they need to foster their intuition.)

I said to Jenna, "I think someone is trying to show us that the outcome can change. Otherwise, I don't feel all three of us would know." I brought her to my office and worked to free up the baby by energetically releasing the tissue restrictions in Jenna's torso. We released as much of the right hip and tissue restrictions as we could.

As soon as her hip freed up, her stomach started to dance. Jenna and I laid hands on her belly as we felt the baby readjust and move down into position. She now no longer looked four months pregnant, she left my office looking and feeling 8 1/2 months pregnant. We both had a good laugh!

We addressed the hip restriction energetically a couple more times before delivery. The good news--it was a short, joyous delivery with minimal pushing thanks to Jenna and her intuition being completely involved. The not-so-good news: We inadvertently proved to the doctor that it really was all "new mom worry."

What do most people think of when they hear the term "natural childbirth"? For some, it is simply synonymous with a vaginal delivery – but without drugs. Do women and their health care providers' understanding of natural childbirth even align with its true definition?

What about all that pain and discomfort? Why do some women experience such unpleasantness and others don't? Do some just get lucky, or do they know something innately -- something other women have not tapped into? So many questions, so little time.

I worked with Lisa, a stay-at home mom who was 8 ½ months pregnant with her second child. Lisa and I had been working together her entire pregnancy. Lisa had a myriad of physical issues from playing youth sports along with being tall and having unstable joints, and pregnancy posed a significant challenge to her. I was able to help her during her pregnancy while addressing issues as they came up. As I started our session on this particular day, I was struck by how different the baby's energy was compared to previous visits.

Typically, when I work on pregnant women, I only work with the mom's energy and I have no idea, energetically, that the baby is there. My understanding is, I help mom and it is mom's job to help the baby. On this day, as I worked with Lisa, all the energetic focus went to the baby's energy. Even more startling, the baby's energy was following the same rhythm and pattern as someone who is getting ready to die. At first, I was shaken. Was the baby in danger? I took a calming breath. Once I realized the baby's energy was shifting, (it was readying itself to soon separate from mom for delivery) I relaxed into it.

When you're getting ready to die, your energy enters into a different vibration you are starting to leave this energy plane and move on to the next. On that day with Lisa, I learned that something similar occurs to a baby's energy when it's preparing for birth. And the best part? This awesome experience didn't end with Lisa. It's an energetic pattern I've observed many times with pregnant women and many people getting ready to pass. Like I talked about in the intro, birth to death are transitions for us. For me I don't see an end, I only see a change in energy. The peace that I experienced know in that we are infinite beings and that birth and death are both new beginning is the most powerful part of this work.

As I continued my session with Lisa and I became aware of the baby's energy focus, the session changed. Lisa went into healing overdrive - focusing her energy on healing some of the physical limitations that would hamper a safe delivery. Issues that had not come up in the past were now on the fore front. This is self-healing at it's most profound moment. There was an incredible shift of space in the abdominal cavity and a realignment of the hip area. Lisa's hips adjusted at that moment to allow the baby to drop into position right there on the table.

It's always amazing to experience the knowing the body has always had. Maybe, you just need a little help remembering by becoming more present in the birthing experience. Most women are present in what they know but not so much what their baby knows. Who was doing all of the work, was it mom or the baby? In any case, Lisa's body knew what needed to happen. I had her focus on the baby, ask it with her mind what it needed, and just hold space energetically. She moved and shifted her body with the direction the baby was giving. All I did was hold energetic space and watched it happen.

Over time, I've learned how to work with moms throughout their pregnancies to help them connect with their baby's energy in the womb. Doing so allows for mom and baby to work together to create the best possible outcome. I strive to make women a part of the process and try to teach them to work with their body and with the baby, not just the pain and contractions. When mom truly connects to her baby, an ongoing conversation is established.

For example, if the baby needs more space, mom can sense this and accommodate: she can do some soft tissue work on herself by stretching and massaging or even just adjust her body position to make herself and the baby work together to make the baby more comfortable. As delivery gets closer, mom is able to work with the baby to get in position and work with the baby through the labor. It's an ongoing energetic dialog. Some women have connected so well that their labor is relatively short, and with little pain and very little pushing. It's all about sitting quiet and listening to what's really going on.

Julie was a strong, successful woman was 8 months pregnant. She learned how to work with her energy and the energy of her baby. She was able to intuitively read her body and prevent a potentially complicated delivery. It unfolded one day when she came in for a visit and told me that her left hip had a lot more tension than the right. And her pelvis was making her feel extremely uncomfortable.

"It feels like the baby is pushing sideways into my pelvis," she explained." I've talked to my doctor about it, but he assured her it was normal pregnancy discomfort." Her face darkened and her voice became firmer. "But I feel very strongly that this is not the case."

How did she know? Did she really know, or was she just uncomfortable and assumed that's what was happening? My take? It's her body. I'll take her word over anyone else's any day. As we worked together that session, it became apparent that Julie's intuition was right. Together, we were able to get an energetic release in the hip area, and as soon as the tissue's restrictions were lifted, the baby started to re-adjust all by itself. Julie just sat quietly and watched her belly move as the baby shifted into a better position.

I've seen this scenario play out with many pregnant women. The only difference is it's never the same restriction with each pregnancy. Which makes sense because no two of us have lived the same life or have the same genetics?

The best gift you can give yourself not only when pregnant but no matter where you are in life is to know yourself and learn what you need to be able to help yourself live a balanced, healthy life.

Why do women have tissue restrictions that hamper normal delivery? Furthermore, why don't you consider tissue restrictions to be an issue? Would an obstetrician or midwife even know about them in the first place? So many questions, so little time.

Meet Karen, a high-powered financial analyst expecting her first child. Karen suffered from severe scoliosis in the lower lumbar region. Her dad, a physician from another country, understood the extent of her scoliosis and knew the natural delivery was going to be a challenge. Karen and her father worked together to find a good obstetrician who would take all issues into account. They found a very reputable doctor at one of the best hospitals in Boston.

Surprisingly, this doctor didn't feel Karen would not have any difficulties delivering naturally. Though her father disagreed, he felt the

doctor must know what's best. Guess her father had strong intuition. He thought to himself 'after all, it's her doctor's specialty, right?' Why did he talk himself out of it? Karen was in the last month of her pregnancy, and the baby was trying to drop down into the pelvis, but the baby ran into an obstacle.

Somehow, due to the pressure of the baby moving into position, it created a hairline fracture in her sacral area. This meant there was no flexibility in the pelvic area or pubic bone so her hips wouldn't open to allow safe passage. Still, her doctor was not alarmed. He chose to believe this development wouldn't impact a natural delivery.

Karen's attempt at a natural delivery didn't go well, and she ended up having an emergency C-section after many hours of trying. Fortunately, she and her baby girl fared well. Now it was time for rehab to follow up with Karen after her C-section. Unfortunately, rehab is not the normal course of treatment after a C-section. This hampered Karen's recovery, not only because it was a C-section, but because she had severe scoliosis. Why wasn't this taken into consideration?

Within three years of trying to regain her life back, her scoliosis degenerated quickly due to the weakness in her abs from her C- section and soon was so bad that her doctors wanted to surgically insert a metal rod along her spine to help support her spine. After working with her to help re-stabilize the lower ab muscles and strengthen her core, scoliosis improved and so far, Karen hasn't needed the surgery.

There has been a lot of research done looking at the weakness of the abdominal area and lower back after a C-section. Now, a lot of progressive hospitals and practices are trying to send women to physical therapy after a C-section to help them regain their prior lower back and abdominal strength. Unfortunately, due to insurance limitations and the lack of knowledge, it's a problem, it's still very limited. Awareness of yourself and what's happening to you and knowing that you have a choice is the ultimate drive for change. So my advice to women is if you have a C-section, ask for physical therapy after and work to get to know your body again after delivery.

Why did I tell you Karen's story? Because there are so many important implications that obstetricians, midwives, doulas, and so forth do not consider when it comes to the female anatomy. Women's bodies are not only being damaged by a C-section but also by the extended amount of time spent pushing during so-called natural childbirth.

I realize one of the reasons there are so many more C-sections being performed is because of the long-term bladder and uterine issues caused by excessive pushing. However, what really needs to happen is an understanding of why women are struggling to deliver naturally and without complications.

My goal is to teach women total body awareness. If you know your body, and you're able to connect with your baby energetically, you can work as a team to create a more positive delivery.

When I meet a woman, who has had a C-section because a vaginal delivery wasn't possible, I ask about the physical traumas she sustained when she was a child or young adult. Most times, lower body injuries such as broken legs, feet, badly sprained ankles, twisted knees or knee surgeries prevent the pelvis from separating at the time of delivery, especially if they happened early in life. This creates tissue restrictions up the legs and creates a rigid pelvis.

If you look at natural childbirth as it's perceived and practiced today, women are pushing for too long. The midwives, doulas, and so forth don't give in until the woman is physically and emotionally spent – or the baby finally comes. Do the practitioners delivering babies have a real understanding of how little a woman should have to push if naturally is really natural?

My friend is an obstetrician/gynecologist, and we were discussing deliveries. I told her how upsetting it was for me to hear stories of mom choosing natural delivery and ending up pushing two, three, and sometimes, four hours. I explained the trauma and side effects on mom's body and the trauma to the baby from pushing so hard against the pelvis. She said the medical community is aware of this; that's why they're opting for the C-section more.

is underway to determine if C-sections lessen the damage to women's bodies long-term. I just want to go on record: Damage is damage – whether it's done surgically or from pushing extensively.

We need to learn why some women are having a hard time delivering naturally, the way the body is designed to do it, not just find another way around the issue. Society has tried to make natural childbirth the norm, the preferred method for delivery. But natural means so much more than what's currently happening in most vaginal births. It has to do with being completely present in your body, not only during delivery but during the pregnancy and also before you even begin to think of getting pregnant. It's about balance and intuition. Just know that you have the power to create the best outcome possible for you and your baby.

The clarity in delivering your child is the child's first step into a balanced or a chaotic life. You have the power as a woman to create balance with your baby's first breath of. How's that for an amazing start in life?

How you come into this world is the first step in your journey -- and it determines how clear your energy is and will be. Babies are coming out of the womb with physical issues they shouldn't have, and this is how blockages and blueprints begin.

If I could speak directly to every woman considering having a baby, I would tell her: Get to know your body first--know yourself. Try yoga before becoming pregnant. If you find you have pretty good flexibility and range of motion, have at it. If you find yoga to be painful, and you've had many soft tissue injuries, look for someone in your area who does integrative manual therapy or keep up with the yoga and support it with massage to gain full flexibility again. This will help you access your body and determine if there are issues that can be addressed before pregnancy.

Also, look for ways to learn intuitive energy healing you can practice yourself. The more in tune you become with yourself versus someone else telling you what to do the better the experience for you and your baby. You can start by trying some of the exercises I've outlined in this book.

Apparently, a study looked at the long-term damage to internal tissue, bladder, and uterus from years of forceps, extensive pushing, and so forth. Now, a study

If you're already pregnant and feel you have restrictions, look for a massage therapist that specializes in pregnancy to gain flexibility and range of motion. Understand what the process is and really try to make the baby part of the process. Sit quietly. Put your hands on your belly and focus on your baby. Ask him/her what they need and wait. You may feel compelled to massage certain tissue areas. Or maybe stretch your hips or back, and so forth. You are not crazy. Your baby's energy will help you, to help him or her.

If you make this a regular practice throughout your pregnancy, you'll find yourself automatically adjusting your body position in the last trimester to accommodate and comfort both you and your baby. This will also tune you into the baby's energy so during labor you can do the same thing. You will know, without anyone coaching you, the best position to put your body in – even if it's not the norm for most women. Know your body. Know yourself. It will completely change your pregnancy and your labor and delivery experience for the better.

The Body Within

CHAPTER 16

How Do You View the World?

I WATCH PEOPLE ALL the time, and I'm amazed that we have no idea how our actions affect those around us. I was at a traffic intersection recently and an oncoming car had the red light. The distracted driver was on her cell phone barreling into the intersection and almost hit a car. The driver of the other car laid on his horn and the cell phone talker finally stopped. But she never looked up, never interrupted her conversation, and never moved the phone in any way.

I don't know about you, but if I'm alerted to stop fast, I instinctively grab onto the wheel with both hands and hit the brakes. I think we call that reaction. Where was her reaction? Why didn't she even flinch at the fact that she almost hurt herself and someone else? No matter who you are, I would think that close of a call deserved a moment of reflection. How could she not see the chaos she just caused?

I had another experience not too long ago that rocked my world and I mean this literally—in that the ground under my feet rocked. I was in my office working on a client and I heard a loud bang. My secretary came running in and said that a car had just crashed into a gas pump at the station across the street. The gas pump was toppled over, and the car and the pump were on fire. I ran to the window just in time to see a Good Samaritan running to the car.

The car was on top of the pump, and its entire right side and the front end was in flames. The Good Samaritan pulled a young girl out of the back, and then the driver out of the front just before the car went up in flames. I was impressed at the clarity of the woman who saved them and how she selflessly put herself in harm's way. After watching this near-death experience, my secretary and I were pretty shaken up.

We watched the car burn as spectators started to surround the scene. My office is about 200 yards away on the second floor right across the street, and I thought, That's a pretty big fire coming out of a gas pump that shows no signs of going out. It was a very old gas station with free-standing pumps and no overhead protection, where newer stations have sprinkler heads in their roofs. Nothing was happening to put out the fire.

I heard someone scream to the gas station attendant, "Shut the gas off! Shut the gas off!" The attendant yelled, "It won't go out!" and the fire continued to burn. Then my secretary turned to me and said, "What if it explodes?" Curiously, my client seemed unfazed and didn't have the same concern. I got nervous and thought maybe we should leave the building and move away from the scene. I looked out the window at the people still standing near the car. I started screaming, "Move away from the car! Was I the only one thinking this might be dangerous?

I ran downstairs to evacuate the building and move everyone away from the area. It was a busy office, and it was business as usual. I ran into the other tenant's office and said, "We should leave the building. They can't put out the fire. We are all in danger." The dentist looked lazily at me. Everyone else in the office was unresponsive and looked at me with confusion and opted to do nothing. I asked the dentist in a calm but stern voice, "Don't you think the fire could ignite the tanks in the ground?" His response: "Hmm, I hadn't thought of that." I continued trying to impress upon him the potential danger. "Don't you think we are too close if something happens?" It almost felt like he was rolling his eyes at me. "Nah, I don't think so," he said and went back to working with his client. Mind you, I could see the scene just across the street as I was talking to him. At that point, I asked myself if I was the crazy one and decided I wasn't.

Just then the fire department arrived. They quickly helped the station owner turn off the pumps and get the fire under control. The whole ordeal was over in about five minutes. I was emotionally spent and overwhelmed by what I had just witnessed. I thought of the little girl and how scary it must have been for her.

I sat for a moment, then broke down. My client, on the other hand, was bewildered by the fact that I let it bother me so much. She couldn't understand why I was so upset and not able to just continue with my day, that I just needed a moment to process it all.

Let's go back to the question "How do we view the world?" Can you witness someone almost die before your eyes and not be affected? I watched my secretary, huddled at her desk, visibly shaking. I was trembling too, yet my client wasn't rattled at all, nor were the people downstairs. Why did the entire office downstairs continue as if nothing terrible was happening fifteen feet away from them? We live in a quiet city; this kind of stuff doesn't happen—ever. Why was there a different interpretation of the same experience? What about the people surrounding the car on fire on top of a gas pump? What was up with that? Was I overreacting? Were they underreacting? I guess we will never know unless the fire had kept burning. That's the hard part about trusting your intuition. If you don't hit the adversity, was it ever real, to begin with? It's kind of like if the tree falls in the forest and there is nobody to hear it fall, did it make noise?

We can apply the same question to other areas of life. Take politics, for example. What one politician thinks is important, two others don't. So how do we find balance in that? What about home life? How many times does the husband think something is important and the wife doesn't? Or, the parent and the child? Who's right? Who's wrong? That, my friends, is where the ability to view what is happening not what we interpret is happening, becomes critically important and life changing.

I wish I could just write one sentence that answers the question, how do we change how we view the world? Unfortunately, I can't. The only thing I can do is to help you break down the barriers that cloud you from seeing what really is, not what you perceive or want it to be.

Why do so many of us want to see things other than what they really are? Let's look at another client, Barbara. Barbara, a stay-at-home wife, and mother was married to the same man for 25 years. They had their ups and downs. She would tell me about some of her friends and how their husbands were verbally abusive and controlling. "I'll never live that way," she said. "What's wrong with them?

After about two years of doing self-work – healing her physical health, cleaning her energy and questioning why she and her friends saw the world the way they did, Barbara had an awakening. She awakened to the reality that she was in an extremely abusive relationship and hadn't seen it. She was living a life that was depleting her emotionally and physically. Barbara had created her own reality that what was happening was completely different than what she saw. Why? It was easier than knowing you are choosing it, so she buried it until she had the strength and tools to see it for what it really was. How's that for a bad dream? Now, what does she do? Most days, she wanted to go back to her bubble. Why? Once you become aware, you have to choose to make changes, live with the pain, or shut back down and let it break you down.

Let me clarify. Barbara chose her reality to protect herself. The good news is as she shifted, so did her husband. They are working together, and their future looks much brighter. That's one reason for living in a created reality. But it's not always about protection. Sometimes, it's fear, ignorance, belief that that's just how life works, or just plain stubbornness and an unwillingness to want to change. It's always easier to stay where you are instead of changing. Other times, it's the way you were taught – until you realize there are many other ways to see it.

Our distorted view of reality is what the Buddhists refer to as life is suffering. Basically, it says that only when you realize you're suffering can you see clearly enough to discover the root of the suffering. Once you discover the root, you have the power to change. But change can only occur if you see and understand the need to change. Healing is about taking off your blinders and seeing yourself completely. Only then can you live in reality. Once this happens, you have the power to create the life that truly makes you happy and at peace.

Here's another example of interpreting your reality. Don was a seemingly healthy, 62-year-old man diagnosed with terminal cancer. Don was a genuinely nice man who I loved to meet with. Don's family was very upset and just couldn't understand how this could happen. They couldn't believe how someone so healthy could get so sick, so fast -- out of nowhere.

Don came to my office and completed a standard intake form, which I read in disbelief. Don's medical history: he had prostate cancer, Type II diabetes, arthritis, heart disease, and so forth. So, this is what Don's family considered healthy? In their view, again, how they saw the situation, all of these health issues were treated, or Don was currently under a doctor's care for them, so they felt that meant he must be healthy. Really?

I have a relative who takes a similar view when it comes to her spouse's health. She called one day to tell me that her husband went to his doctor, and they gave him a clean bill of health, "He's all healed up," she said. I scratched my head. Let's see, he can't breathe very well or walk any distance, he's tired all the time, and has a bad heart, and so forth. I'm glad he's so healthy. My relative interpreted the doctor's evaluation as her husband's fine. I cleared my throat. "He's as healthy as one can be in his condition." Her response, "You make issues where there are none. The doctor said he is healthy." What could I say to that?

When you only see what you want to see in each situation, you're helpless when things don't go as planned. My relative is always surprised when her spouse has an infection or ends up in the hospital. "How could this happen?" she asks. What kind of solution can you come up with if you don't want to see the problem? How can you fix something that's not right if you choose for it to not be there? There's nothing to fix if you can't see it, right? Oh, then it's not your fault. You're just a victim of life.

Going back to Sam and Mary, how much of the distortion was because nobody really understood the situation clearly? Hence, the doctors and the patients made it what they wanted it to be which, ultimately, limited the possible outcomes. Just look around you. How do you view the world around you? How do your children view the world?

Now that I'm a grandmother, I'm able to take the time to observe the parent-child relationship without being in it. I remember when my grandson, Zack, was about 12 months old, and his dad would be using his laptop. Zack would do a couple of things to get his dad's attention, but Dad wouldn't budge so that Zack would slap the keyboard. That would get Dad's attention. This became how Zack got Dad's attention. So, how did this child know if that was good attention or bad attention? Is it because we tell them it's good or bad? Is there good attention and bad attention? Zack just wanted Dad to notice him, and his father did. So, how does Zack now perceive his actions and when does his perception change? How will he get attention in school? With his peers?

The gist of it: you completely create how you view the world and how your children view the world.

I challenge you to really question how you are viewing the world. Do you see it like everyone else sees it? Do you have a different opinion on issues? Do your kids share your opinion because it's yours? Or is it theirs? Why do you see it different? Is there maybe, a bit of distortion in how you see it? Keep asking yourself questions and observe your kids' actions. I bet it's like looking in a mirror. The question is, is it a clean mirror or a mucky one?

As you start to see the world around you for what it is, not what you have chosen to see it, this brings more balance and healing to your energy. As you bring more balance, your intuition comes in clearer, so you are more connected to *The Body Within*. This now gives you more tools with making better choices regarding chronic pain and health issues.

I see many people get excellent advice from various sources that would help their situation, but according to them, it won't work. They have not investigated it or even tried it--they just already have a strong opinion of if its right or not. Unfortunately, I have seen clients throw away what I call their miracle (advice from others, jobs in their path, their own intuition, opportunities, health advice, etc.) because in the world they live in, the answer has no value that has come their way.

I'd like to see you break through your beliefs that you can't do this and sit quietly daily with the mini-me exercise in Chapter 6 and ask to see what you need to see. This will open you up to seeing if you live in reality or a created reality. Think of the healing possibilities if there really are more options than what you believe you have now.

CHAOS BREEDS CHAOS,
BALANCE BREEDS PEACE

The Body Within

CHAPTER 17

Creating Your Own Reality

"You can create your own reality to make life what you want it to be, but you can't create reality. Reality just is."

WHAT DOES "Reality just is" REALLY MEAN?

Let's take a look at some examples of how people can create their own realities.

Ten years ago, a close friend of mine was working full-time at a retail store. She was planning to have her third hernia surgery in 18 months, and she also had a myriad of other health issues. My intuition was in overdrive. I knew if she had another surgery so soon there would be a very bad outcome later in her life. I tried to make her understand the damage she was doing to her body, and how she really needed to take a step back to try and rectify the situation.

I kicked into protective mode and went to her doctor's appointments with her. I also got her husband involved to coordinate a treatment plan after surgery that would focus on core strengthening and stability training. I absolutely knew if she had this surgery and went right back to work she would not only get hurt again, but the long-term consequences would be devastating. I knew in my gut that her bad habits (not taking care of herself, excess weight and lifting when she shouldn't be, and so forth) and lack of respect for her body were going to catch up with her in a bad way. Still, I felt she had plenty of time to correct it.

The plan was for her to take four or five months off from work and do the rehabilitation her body desperately needed to heal. Her husband agreed, even though it would be costly due to lost wages and having to pay health insurance. The surgeon was on board, and my friend even had her own physiatrist (a Doctor of Physical Therapy) in charge of her care. Everything was in place. She had the surgery, and we were moving forward with the agreed-upon plan.

That is, until my friend went to her four-week post-op appointment, without me this time, and told the surgeon she was fine and ready to go back to work. She said she wasn't interested in the rehab program and refused all help. Because physical therapy was not a normal treatment for hernia surgery. Her doctor gave her a note clearing her and back to work she went. Of course, I was furious and didn't know how to handle it. My gut was on fire, and I knew she had just made a really bad choice with dire consequences down the road. I knew in my heart she should be the one making choices for her, but I also knew she was not one to pay attention to her body, so this decision was not good. Ten years later, three more surgeries, and one extra large belly infection, my friend has no abdominal muscles left to support her core and lower back. She can barely walk any distance, and her quality of life is very limited at the age of 72. And every day she wants to know, "Why did this happen to me?"

Did any of this have to happen? Do you think she even knows she chose to be in this situation? Is this any different than the person who knows their cholesterol is high but refuses to do anything about it, then, voila -Here comes the diagnoses: heart disease, bypass surgery, and type 2 diabetes? Then it's, "Poor me. Why did this happen?" What about yourself? Take a hard look in the mirror at the health choices you're making right now.

I ask clients all the time to do some basic exercises to help their body heal. I tell them, "If there's anything you can find the time for, it should be core strengthening." Your core (abdominal muscles) supports your gait, your lifting, pulling, sitting, standing, climbing stairs, healthy aging, and so forth. Most clients say they're too busy, or they're just not interested.

Then one day they go outside, maybe do a little yard work, play some golf, and they get hurt. All because they didn't have the stability to use their body the way they wanted to. As a practitioner, you hope the bells go off, and they start to take better care of themselves, but it's usually not the case.

I tell people all the time, "You can't expect change if no change happens." You make choices that define the direction your life takes.

You may want to take a good look in the mirror and see if you are really viewing life and yourself from a clear perspective. Do you see your spouse for who he/she is or who you think he/she are? What about your kids? Are they really the star on the soccer team or just an average player? And yourself? Now there's a tough one. Are you really an exemplary employee who's doing everything perfectly at work, and the boss just has a personal vendetta against you? Are you the over-doer at work in hopes you will be noticed (exhausting yourself in the process)? Are you the friend that takes or are you the friend that gives all the time? Mirror, mirror, mirror. Every time you take a moment to observe yourself and others, you're now in the moment and not two steps ahead in your thoughts and reactions. This is how you begin to see yourself and the world a lot clearer.

The best example I can give of creating your own reality is with my daughter, Janice, and her fiancé, Justin were expecting a baby. Janice was a student in her third year of college and a little naïve. Justin was overly confident, tall, handsome, with a loving but often confusing side. Justin liked to make life what he wanted it to be. He would always have a predetermined outcome for almost every situation and most times things never worked out as he planned. As the pregnancy progressed, they would talk about how they wanted to deliver the baby. They were using a midwife and wanted a drug-free, natural birth. Since Janice was a nursing student and Justin's mom was a nurse, I asked them what their plans were in the delivery room.

"We're not going to take the classes. They told us we would have a nurse with us the entire time to help us through it."

I suggested they might want to do more research and understand birthing positions, the labor process, and so forth. Their response: "We've got it all figured out. The nurse is going to help us with that, too." Oh really, I thought. The next decision for them was who would be with them when the baby was born. Janice wanted me to do energy work throughout the delivery. Justin was not on board with the energy work and said I could be there as long as I leave just before the baby was born so they could have that moment together.

I smiled and said to them, "I can be there as a practitioner, or I can be there as Grandma and to offer support and love, and when the baby is being born, I will leave. "Or," I told them, "I don't have to be there at all."

They chose the second option. Janice knew she couldn't have it both ways and as much as she knows the possibilities in my work, selling Justin on it was not going to happen. Together, we decided this was best. Then, the fun began.

Janice went into labor. Now, remember, I'm Grandma who's had three C-Sections, never full labor and delivery. My work is quite different. I wasn't well-versed in the conventional teachings for breathing and positions during childbirth. I helped the best I could, and lo and behold; there was no nurse to walk us through anything. Justin didn't know how to comfort Janice. He hadn't done any research and intuitive he was not. Janice knew some of the positions, but she couldn't focus to help us help her. The contractions were strong and coming fast, but they weren't productive.

This went on for about four hours. I knew the labor was stalled, but remember, my role was Grandma. Why didn't I interfere at that point? First and foremost, I knew he would not let me and second, I did not want to get thrown out of the room. My intuition kept saying, Wait, it's not time yet. But as her mom and Grandma, I wanted to shake them both like rag dolls. The midwife came to check Janice, and she was only at three centimeters. No progression. She decided to medicate Janice so she could sleep through the labor and, hopefully progress.

While Janice slept for a couple of hours, Justin's mother, Maureen, showed up. Maureen was a strong, confident woman who was a nurse who had a close, but complicated relationship with her son.

Janice woke up, the midwife checked her, and there was still no progression. They began discussing whether to continue on this path or give Janice Pitocin to progress labor aggressively. That was my cue. At that moment, I said, very loudly, so everyone could hear, "Or..." Maureen asked, "Or, what?" I explained what I could do to help, and as I was explaining, Justin yelled, "We agreed. You're not to get involved." Maureen sent her son out of the room and asked Janice, "Do you think your mother can help?" "Yes," Janice replied. Maureen looked puzzled but said to Janice, "It's your body, not his. You get to choose, but Pitocin would be my last choice. What do you want to do?" I gave Grandma-to-be a big smile. Then Janice tiredly whispered, "Mom, please help me."

I was able to help balance her energy to help her body restart labor in about 15 minutes. Janice was ready to push in about 45 minutes. Once she was pushing, the baby's head was about to crown. At that moment, I realized Justin's wish for everyone to leave the room when the baby was delivered was not going to happen. The baby boy was born with the cord wrapped around his neck but cried right away, so Mom was not worried. While Justin went with the midwife and the baby, I stayed behind to help Janice finish with the cleanup. Everything calmed down, and the midwife brought my grandson to his mother's waiting arms. Mom, Dad, and their new baby, it was amazing to watch. As I was packing up and leaving, Justin stopped me as I was almost out the door. He gave me a big hug and a smile. "Please stay."

Do you think they ever really wanted the first moments alone? If so, why did they want me there at all? I've actually had a couple of clients tell me that same scenario. Mom and Dad-to-be wanted Grandma in the room until the baby was ready to be born, but then they wanted that moment alone. Why not do the whole thing alone then? I think I call that conditional support. Do as I say, not as I need. Is there any room for intuition there?

If Janice and Justin had done more homework, they would have had more tools to help each other. Isn't it funny how they planned every moment? Can you really plan life if you're going to live? They thought they would have a nurse and a midwife available to them the entire time, and they felt that was such a better option than what Janice has always known and used intuitively. Why did she veer away from her truth to please him?

I was the observer and never interfered until it was needed. All the support they believed was going to be there was not, and the support they didn't want to acknowledge was. For me, it was like a movie playing out to give my daughter a chance to choose her truth with Justin and the accepted norms of society.

What do you think happened to Janice energetically at the moment she asked for my help? What happened to Justin when he totally changed his tune and wanted me to stay? Was he sincere? Yes, he was.

I can honestly say everything that happened to Janice and Justin set us up for the next couple of weeks because of their baby, Zack, ended up needing emergency surgery. Had they not grown through this childbirth experience, the baby's outcome, later, would have been completely different. A little growth goes a long way.

Janice was not the strongest person when she met Justin. After their life experiences together, with a lot of ups and downs along with many more moments for Janice to choose her truth. Now, she is now a very strong, realistic, open-minded observer -- and a hell of a nurse. So, was Justin a bad choice or a good choice for her? Adversity in life—sometimes you create it, sometimes it just happens. That's what life is.

My goal for you is when adversity does happen, you have the tools to help yourself. Life will always teach you if you allow it.

CHAPTER 18

Master Teacher

RITA WAS IN HER late 50s and a very caring person. She lived a very healthy lifestyle but had been struggling with a patch of skin cancer on her right cheek for many years. Her prognosis was not good. She was scheduled for a radical surgery to remove the cancer, leave the wound open, and continue doing surgery until there were clean margins. Rita's doctor told her that she would be very disfigured by the time the desired outcome was achieved, but he would do his best.

I saw Rita a month before the scheduled surgery and was able to see that, for some reason, her energy was very imbalanced, and her body was not aware of cancer energetically. To me, I interpret that is her body detached from that part of her body and could no longer see it to heal it. In my experience, this isn't always the case with cancer. We all have different pasts, genetic make-ups, and lifestyles. Not knowing why or how or if this even had anything to do with her illness, I allowed myself to be guided. By the end of the first session, I could tell that her body had reconnected the flow. The body was now aware of cancer on her cheek. Her energy was working in her favor.

I was happy for her but also distressed because I couldn't share this with her for several reasons. What if I was wrong? And if I was right, how could I prove it? I knew in my gut she had been doing self-healing work for a long time, and she had made tremendous progress in healing herself. My work just pulled it all together.

After Rita had left my office, she had an appointment with her doctor. He was as distressed about the upcoming surgery as she was. He asked her to try an experimental cream for a couple of weeks to see what would happen. She came back for her third session, and I knew things were really getting better, but I still wasn't comfortable sharing my knowing with her.

You see, my work is a complement to medicine. As I do my self- taught energy work, I work with the individual to help them heal themselves physically, emotionally, and spiritually. I guide the individual into finding and embracing their own healing. As I explained in Chapter 5 about psychics, I can only read your energy at that moment. If you make different choices when you leave my office, that outcome or energy imprint I read can change directions. My goal is to help you know yourself and how your choices affect your healing. By listening to *The Body Within*, you will know if your healing is prevailing or not long before the doctors tell you.

She called me a couple of days later to tell me the results of a biopsy performed a week earlier. She explained that a lab had been growing cells to see how aggressive her cancer was. "Everyone is shocked," she told me, obviously elated. "The cancer isn't growing. It's reversing itself. The cream is working."

I was happy for Rita. The cancer was healing. I knew Rita was healing herself, not the cream. She was in tune with her body and was making choices specific to her and her healing. She wasn't giving away her personal power any longer. With her big heart, she had been caring so much for others, she didn't take care of herself enough. As she claimed back herself and finally recognized her value and importance, she progressed rapidly. She was her own healer and had been long before I met her. I was helping her pull it all together.

I talk about how every experience gives us tools so when we are faced with similar things again, we are not helpless--we can tap into the endless possibilities in healing. Fast forward five years, and the dear friend and colleague who had referred Rita called me. Alice was a middle-aged, slightly anxious, very open-minded and a caring person. She told me that she had just been diagnosed with an aggressive skin cancer on her right cheek, and the doctor wanted to do a radical surgery. I was shocked. She asked if I thought I could help her. Alice said her doctor prescribed a cream to try. He said it was a long shot, but he had seen it work once before. He had hoped Alice would have similar results.

I know what you're thinking. I must have helped Alice, and she was cured just like Rita. Wrong. This is the part where life teaches and the art of intuition, observation and listening gives you the correct answer - not the answer you want.

As our conversation continued, I refreshed Alice's memory about Rita. I told Alice that Rita was this doctor's other cream patient. Naturally, she was thrilled. This meant I could cure her, too. I took a deep breath, and said: "Alice, have the surgery." She was floored. She asked me, "Why won't you heal me like you did Rita?" That was Alice's answer. She wanted me to fix her. I explained to Alice that ever since I'd known her, she had never healed from inside. Rather she was always on the bandwagon, gathering quick fixes and empty promises. "If I thought for one second you had the commitment and self- discipline to heal yourself, I would help you, but there's too much at stake to hope for change." I took a breath, then continued, "I would be more than happy to help you with your post-surgery recovery," and I did. We were both please when she had a successful outcome.

Life is the best teacher you have. I call life, my Master Teacher, and Mentor. Some nights, my daughter Janice, who is a nurse, comes over. We sit at the dining room table, have a glass of wine, and discuss life. I think of the endless teaching Janice is exposed to daily, working on a medical surgery floor of a 200-bed hospital. Janice has not only learned from her parents but also from her time with her son Justin, her work, and so forth. I kid around with her some days saying, "Soon enough, you'll be teaching me." We both smile, realizing that, as time passes, we're less mother and daughter and more mentors to each other.

My second child, Molly, is growing more and more each day. This energy sensitive daughter is the most like me. Beautiful and smart, witty, and fun, she sometimes has trouble adapting to new situations. Molly can feel and sense the energy people give off, not always knowing how to handle it. I had the same issues when I was young, so the way I was taught to handle it was to get sent into the fire. I had no advice, I just had to handle it. Well, years of lacking self-confidence and fearing others taught me not to do this to her. Again, this is life as the Master Teacher.

When Molly was younger, I started off by letting her sit on my lap and observe everyone in the room. I explained who everyone was and let her ask questions and come to her own conclusions. From about the age of two to six, it took her anywhere from fifteen minutes to three hours before she felt comfortable in a new situation.

Then came school age. She did okay, but the first month of every school year was a struggle. Every new teacher and all the new kids around her were a struggle. Not once did I tell her to get over it. I knew what she was going through. Through trial and error, I learned to help her not repeat my history. I knew if I could help her understand her thoughts and how they were affecting her experiences, she wouldn't have to struggle so much later in life trying to figure it all out.

Today, Molly has many different skills and is the most independent of my three children. We are best friends just as I am with my oldest but in a very different way. Janice helps me deal with life. Molly helps me be stronger in who I am, to love who I am, and who I'm becoming more every day. So, some days I'm the teacher, and some days I'm the student. How wonderful is that? This is a perfect example of how life teaches.

I read many parenting books when my kids were little. I remember learning to use intuition and discern what my children needed, and when they needed to graduate from one stage to another.

I was blessed to use intuition as my children transitioned from one stage to the next. I remember the bottle was gone as soon as they could hold a cup. The key was if they needed it, it was okay, but if you let them have it past the need stage, they would become emotionally attached. Then it would be much more difficult for them to let go. It was the same with silverware, walking, transitioning to a bed or bedtime, and so forth.

At each stage of development, if you could just read your children, and what they need, not want, they would just let go when you introduced the next milestone. This taught me so much about watching and listening. They didn't have a bottle past eight months, they walked at ten months, and were in beds at a year. There were no pacifier issues, and so forth. I was never mean about it; they ultimately chose it. They just didn't know it at the time.

Now, I watch new mom's struggle. It's not about reading the child and using their instincts. It's about what the doctors say, what the books say, or what's convenient for the parents. They are not using intuition to see what their child needs.

If you're a parent, I challenge you to look at your child as an individual. See him or her for who they are and what they need specifically, not what they want and know. So many parents parent the way they were parented, or in contrast, boycott the way they were raised. Or they live by something they read. Are they just teaching kids to see another fake reality? Let life be your Master Teacher. Help your kids see what's really happening around them, so they will have tools to handle life and its adversity, and you'll gain more tools as well.

Your life experiences teach you how to parent your children, so be sensitive to what is happening in society with kids, schools, and peer pressure. When it comes down to it, you are your child's parent and you being sensitive to your child's needs, and parent according to those needs, will empower your child to grow, and learn, and be independent. You are their teacher, not their savior.

I had a friend who said her child would never have a cell phone. She felt strongly about its negative influence. I agreed with her but asked how her daughter would handle not having a phone and being the outcast at school. She said those ever-popular words: "She'll be fine. She'll get over it." I smiled and asked, "Is your daughter strong in who she is, or is she insecure?" She repeated, "She's fine. It has nothing to do with that. She just doesn't need a phone."

So, then I asked about Mom's high school experience. "Were you strong or insecure?" I asked. Not surprisingly, Mom replied, "It's not about that. Society is out of control, and I don't think she should have a cell phone." Maybe, the better approach was for Mom to give her daughter a phone but put parental controls on it and help her understand the risks and benefits and how to use it properly. Use your knowledge to help your kids choose a better path in life. It may not happen in the first week they have a phone, but you'll see, in time, they'll figure it out if you give them the tools.

Mom's point was valid, but she didn't consider the effects on her child because, in her mind, it didn't matter. Now, if she listened to the news and paid attention to topics like peer pressure, bullying, and teen depression, do you think she might have taken a different approach -- one that didn't isolate her daughter from her peers? Life is happening to her daughter even if Mom lives in a chosen reality.

The point I'm trying to make is that life teaches. When you make a decision that will affect you or someone else, you should also look at the effects of the choice from different angles. As soon as you ask yourself, "What is the effect of my choice?" you have to learn a new way of thinking and only then will you realize how big that choice is. In thinking this way, it will open so many more possibilities on how you live, how you heal, and how you age.

As I use Life is the Master Teacher every day, I'm humbled by things I witness. This is another great example: I have a client and friend who came to me when his dad was dying. Paul, middle-aged, successful, and with a kind heart loved his dad, Steve, but didn't do well under this kind of stress. When his dad started to really fail, Paul told me he wasn't going back to see his dad. He wanted to remember him the way he was.

I felt love for Paul and his father and hoped I could share that with my friend. "Paul, I'm very sorry about your dad, but it's not about you." I looked at my friend. "How do you think your dad is feeling right now? He is the one dying. How do you think he will feel if you don't show up for him?" He said again, "I don't want to remember him that way. It's better this way." I then started questioning him about how his mom and sisters were acting around his dad. He said they were poking and prodding, and basically, driving him nuts. "Well, that really sucks for your dad," I said. "You have a great sense of humor. He adores you and admires your clearheaded thinking. Yet, you're going to let him die with a bunch of women fussing over him pretending he's not dying. What a way to go."

Paul was very quiet after that, and I wasn't sure how he would handle it, but I said what I said for his dad — and for him. My goal was to break the pattern in Paul's thoughts — to get him to step outside his fear so that he could see another possibility in the situation.

Now, here comes the humbling part. Paul came back and told me that he had been hanging out with Steve and he broke the ice by making a Top 10 list for his dad to take with him when he meets God. I guess we can thank David Letterman for that one. It was great. I still smile every time I think about it. Paul found a way to make it better, not only for his dad but himself, as well. Paul's dad went from not being able to talk about dying to having it all in the open. More importantly, Steve's fears about dying diminished and his crossing over was peaceful.

Why is death so hard for us to deal with and talk about? Death is a major part of life. If you take all the experience you've had in life that pertains to death, it gives you tools. Take these tools to re-visit how you feel about death and do you see it with clarity. I used to be terrified of death. It wasn't until I started this work that I went back to my first memory and I realized death was not how I saw it. I was very young and the only thing I knew was my grandfather died. No one talked and everyone was sad. We went to this big place and they shot off guns that made everyone cry. Then, for a long period of time, my parents didn't talk, everything was different. How could I have seen it any other way till I started to sit with each experience and started to see some of the beauty and not the pain and the fear? I know unexpected death can be a terrible tragedy, but not all death is that way. Instead of having one opinion about death, let each experience form your opinion. Think of all the blueprints or muck you can clear.

As life plays out, we all face death at one time or another. Sometimes it's a loved one, sometimes a friend, even your pets will die. Some deaths are quick and unexpected, some are the result from a long illness. No matter the reason, every person dies. Life teaches you that you can accept the reality in front of you, or you can pretend something else is happening. Holding on to grief from a pet or loved one can really have an effect on your overall health and well-being. You owe it to yourself to learn how to be strong in who you are so when you lose someone close. It is a loss but not a disability.

When my mother-in-law Grace was dying, my children were informed every step of the way and weren't shocked when their grandmother eventually died. My kids went to see her in the hospital and as they came out of the room, one by one, they put their arm around me and said, "Mom, it's okay. She's ready. She needs to go now. "I had kept them up-to-date on what her doctors said, and when she started to fail. I never kept bad news from them. I told them the truth and let them ask as many questions as they needed to. This not only helped them, but it helped me see things clearer, as well.

Another family member, Barbara, took the opposite approach Barbara has always seen life as she needed it to be for her own safety rather than as it is, so now she was protecting her children from how sick Grace was. They were 14 and 16 and had no real understanding of the process of death. They had no tools and didn't understand the extent of their grandmother's illness. The night Grace died, I took my kids and Barbara's to the hospital café for dinner. The 16-year-old asked me when Grammie was coming home. I took a deep breath and said "I'm not sure what you know, but Grammie is not coming home. I'm very sorry, but she's very ill and will probably die tonight."

They didn't want to believe me. They just didn't understand what was going on. They asked me several more questions, which I answered truthfully. However, they chose not to believe me. No one else had explained all of this to them, so how could this be? They thought she was fine. My kids tried to help them, but it wasn't their reality. They could only process so much information at once. We went back upstairs to Grace's room, and she died within an hour. The 16-year-old was so shocked and distraught that she screamed in the hallway. We had to pull her to a private area, and it took her hours to calm down.

Why did this have to happen? Did the parents not know Grace was really that sick? Or didn't they want to believe it? If they chose not to believe it, how could they tell their kids what was happening? They were not acknowledging previous experiences to help them with their, present and not using life as a Master Teacher. It didn't exist in their world. If, as parents, you don't want to accept what's happening, how can you help your kids? How will this affect their view of death in the future along with the pain they carry every day in their body and mind?

Sometimes, one person's inability to face life and what's really happening not only impacts them, but it causes a chain of events for those around them. That's why we're all in the dark to some degree. We started out life as clear souls and then, our parents, relatives, and society teach us about life. Do we begin to choose what we believe to be true or just believe what they tell us? As I talked about in Chapter 6, that's how blueprints are established.

Everything that happens to you is an experience. You can choose to learn from it, or you can choose just to let life pass you by. I tell people all the time, "If it comes your way – even if it's a homeless person on the street – take a second and reflect. If you feel bad, feel bad. If you feel angry, feel angry. If you feel happy, feel happy and then ask yourself, "Why do I feel this way?"

What this does is help you quantify your thoughts. It helps you realize how you view the world. Most people just react with a thought or emotion but don't dig deeper to understand the roots of it. When you really ask, why, you start to truly understand who you are. That, my friends, is how life teaches.

The Body Within

CHAPTER 19

Answers

EVERY TIME YOU READ something or are exposed to something new, ask yourself, is it my truth or not? Do you embrace answers, or do you discard them without consideration because they don't fit with the way you perceive life? I'm equally guilty. When someone gives me advice and it's not what I want to hear, the wall goes up, and I never knew the advice was my answer all along.

When my husband was out of work, he would search for jobs on the computer, send his resume off into the unemployment abyss, and hope for a response. Meanwhile, I would come home with job leads, or someone else would give him a tip, but he wouldn't follow up on it. When I asked why, he would say, "It doesn't work that way. Companies don't want you to send a resume if they're not posting a job." I would say, "If it comes your way, follow through on it. What do you have to lose? Answers come in many packages, just like motorcycles." Do you see the connection - or disconnect - in his vision? You're given answers to your questions and problems daily. You just can't see them because they don't look or sound like a Harley. Luckily for me, with my husband, if I poke a few times, he starts to see the possibilities in front of him and things start to open. For a lot of people, that is not the case. That is why a lot of people my age all struggle with their aging parents. They try to help them but t h e lifetime of not seeing the possibilities around them leaves them very blocked and a lot of times, very stubborn in their later years. This creates a lot of stress and worry for the children caring for them and a lot of time on unnecessary suffering in their everyday living. The sooner you can learn to be open, the less likely it will be a problem as you age. Then, as you age and problems arise, the answer will be right in front of you rather than you fighting a created reality that has no answers.

Let's go back in time a bit when I needed shoulder surgery, I got three opinions. Two doctors told me the surgery was risky and not always a good outcome. I wanted the surgery because I was in pain, impatient, and just had it in my head that it would work. I wanted the surgery to be my answer. So, I persevered and got a third opinion which was, "It's an easy surgery. I do it all the time, and I have a great success rate." That was what I wanted to hear. So, I did the surgery without giving it a second thought. As I talked about, it didn't turn out so well. The surgeon ended up nicking a nerve and paralyzing muscles in my shoulder, which created a lot of right-sided dysfunction.

Could I have seen this coming? Remember, two other doctors felt it was too risky. So, why did I feel the third doctor knew better? Did I use my gut? Heck no. I didn't even know I had a gut back then. Instead, I discovered that if I push hard enough, I can get anything I want. Just like our stubborn elderly. What I didn't understand back then is what I <u>want</u> isn't always what I <u>need</u>. It was a very hard lesson for me to learn. Do I regret it? Again, heck no. Why not? Because it made me who I am today.

Answers come in many packages.

Dreams are one. Dreaming is a great way to ask for help. Sit quietly before you go to bed and ask for an answer to come in a dream. It may take a few nights, and sometimes you will remember it. Other times, you remember getting the answer, but don't remember the dream. It will come--just be patient.

Intuition is another. Intuition, a strong knowing, is how most of us get answers. The more you clear away your muck, the stronger the answers become.

Synchronicity is another. A series of events just keeps showing up unexpectedly to help you see what you need to see. Then when all the pieces connect, you get what I call your miracle.

People in your life. It could be doctors, teachers, parents, friends, clergy, and even total strangers. You never know the package. Just stay open.

Here's another example from my own life that gave me answers. At the time, I was having a disagreement with my mom. I try not to let her get to me, but this time she did, and I held onto the anger that I wouldn't normally attach to our disagreements. I was out running errands and stopped at the grocery store. An elderly woman was struggling to unzip her coat, so I stopped to help. As I helped with her zipper, she looked confused. Then she realized where she was, thanked me, and went on her way. I didn't give it a second thought until our paths crossed again in the store. She stopped to ask me where they moved the produce department. They didn't move it. She just couldn't find it. At that moment, I knew. With all people in that store, why was I the one to see her distress? Not once, but twice. I went home and said to my husband, "Someone is trying to tell me to let the argument go. My mom's old and she does not see life as clearly as she used to." I did what my gut told me to do and tried to let it go. Three days later, I was with my mom, and she had an episode that lasted about five minutes. She argued with me about something that happened when she was younger. It was obvious she thought I was someone from her past, and that what she was upset about was happening now. She was confused and not present. I was stunned. Back in that grocery store, the message came in the perfect package. Even though I acknowledged it, I only saw part of the message until the rest played out. I was sad to see my mom's life heading in this direction, but I was happy to know I wasn't walking alongside her alone—I had intuitive messages that help me support her.

I also get a lot of my answers in dreams or visions – with a very strong intuition or knowing. As I work with clients to help them clear their energy field, this opens them up to more possibilities and aids in their overall healing. Some clients start to dream or have visions. Some develop stronger intuition, and some just become more confident in their knowing. It all depends on their soul's journey. Whatever their soul's strengths are -- that's what gets stronger. There's no specific way for any one person to heal. So many people want the process to be cut and dried -- to get an answer from something outside themselves. A doctor, parent, teacher, friend, and so forth can be your "answer" just as much as your own intuition. Answers are everywhere. The more you become in tune with your surroundings, the more you see, hear and feel your answers.

As I said, dreams play a big part in how I get my answers. Dreams give me yet another tool to work with in dealing with life. I'm going to share a few of my dreams because I want you to know that being aware is not finding bliss and peace for yourself. It's about being aware of what's happening around you and the many tools available to help you handle life. Think of dreams as the same as being a good observer. If you're aware of what's going to happen and you see everyone and everything clearly, without blinders, you always know what's going to happen next. I saw the woman in the store as old and frail. I didn't want to see the true reality of my mom's situation. But once I did, I found peace in an otherwise sad situation. I stopped fighting my reality and sat in it. Peace comes with the release of the fight.

Another example of seeing reality you may have observed is watching a loved one go down a self-destructive path. When you get the phone call that they're in the ER and it doesn't look good, you're not surprised. You saw it coming. Of course, you're upset, but not shocked. There's no confusion, and you don't fall victim to, why is this happening? How could this be? Dreams do the same thing for you. It doesn't make it easier knowing, but it gives you a heads up. And it helps you understand you choose your own path.

Here's an example of my own shifting. I had a dream that was extremely unsettling. At the time, my daughter, Janice, was 4 ½ months pregnant. In my dream, I could see her vividly. She was there with the baby and the baby's father. Every time they fed the baby, the food fell out of his mouth. I kept hearing, "The baby can't eat." The only explanation I could come up with was that the baby would be born with a cleft palate or similar condition. This is where I get into trouble with my intuition. I always have to have a logical explanation rather than waiting to see what happens. The baby 'couldn't eat' wasn't enough for me; I had to give it a diagnosis.

Throughout the pregnancy, I periodically shared my concerns with Janice that the baby was going to have something wrong with it. "He's not going to be able to eat," I told her. "That's all I know." At first, I didn't want to tell her, but my gut kept saying, she needs to know. At times, she took me seriously and put it in the background and hoped I was wrong – so did I - but at other times, she would just say, "Yeah. I feel the same way, but I am not sure if it's just new mom worry." I knew from experience to stay strong and confident in what you know, and it will eventually play out. It may be a day, month or even a year later, but it will play out.

Delivery day came, and our perfectly healthy, beautiful baby boy Zack was born. Janice and I looked at each other. I smiled and said, "I guess I was wrong this time." Happy day! The next day, I spoke to Janice several times. Zack still hadn't taken to nursing. That evening she called to say Zack was undergoing tests at the hospital to try and determine why he couldn't nurse.

I hung up the phone, rushed to the hospital and sat with the new parents. I had a minute alone with Janice and I asked her, "What's your gut telling you?" She said, "Something's wrong – I always felt it from the time I was pregnant, even before you said something. I just did not want it to be real, but he's going to be okay." Feeling nervous and calm and the same time, I reached for her hand. "Why do you feel it is going to be okay?" She said, "I'm concerned, but I'm not scared. I know, Mom, I just know." She asked me if I felt that all would be okay, and I answered, "The dream said he couldn't eat, not that he was going to die. My gut feels good. I'm not sure what it could be but let's go with that."

Within three hours, we were being rushed to Dartmouth-Hitchcock Medical Center in Lebanon, NH. Tests had revealed that Zack's large and small intestines were not connected. Both the small and large intestines were closed--dead ends. We were told it was a very rare condition, but it could be fixed. "He couldn't eat," was the only information I received. How could I know this was the diagnosis? My gut knew I was right, but my brain? My brain wanted more. Let's just say, I'm a work in progress.

Zack had surgery to reattach the intestines and today he is a perfectly healthy little boy. Is he perfect because the surgery was a success and the doctors fixed him completely? No. They did the surgery, Zack healed, but then scar tissue became an issue. Janice, who is now a nurse, watched for signs and kept bringing him to me. We tag teamed him, using intuitive energy and bodywork for the first two years of his life.

Essentially, we read what Zack needed and worked with his body to correct issues as they arose. Fortunately, Zack also has an open- minded pediatrician who has helped him heal with some Alternative means. The really neat thing about this story is that there wasn't just one answer, but many answers, from multiple modalities that worked together to help Zack. I picked the brains of many Alternative and Western practitioners and used a great deal of intuition. My daughter was also trusting of the process. Her openness, her lack of fear, and her ability to make decisions for her son, using all types of medicine still amazes me. I was 46, and just finding that moxie. I love her for that.

On that note, I challenge those of you in the Alternative and Western medicine worlds to consider becoming allies to one another rather than an adversary. Set aside the immediate judgment and reach out to learn what the other knows. Without many modalities of medicine, this child would not have the life he has today. Ask yourself, what is it inside me that makes me feel my answer is superior to those of others?   Why do I feel negative toward others? Is it because of what you've read, what you think, what you believe? In all the years I have done this work, I have equally as many good and negative stories about Western and Alternative medicine. I guess that means they both need to work on what they know, so you need to work on being more present to navigate medicine as a whole. If you sit quietly and ask, I promise, you will get an answer over time. It just may not be in the package you want it in.

Western medicine has divided the body up into so many sections that you don't know how to put it back together. By the same token, Alternative Medicine needs to see the limitations of what they can do and add it to the strengths of Western Medicine. There needs to be less criticizing of each other and more respect for what the other brings to the table. When it comes to a practitioner helping a patient, it should be about critical thinking, not personal preferences. If you're a practitioner reading this and a patient comes in already being treated the opposite of what you treat, feel your internal reaction to what they say. Do you listen with an open mind? Or is your response to shut the patient down? Did you miss an opportunity to learn from the patient? Think about it. Answers are everywhere.

Another way to get answers is to watch life as it plays out. While my grandson was at Dartmouth Hospital, mistakes were made with his care. Not life-threatening mistakes, but critical ones none-the- less. After performing this life-saving surgery, the estimate was it could take seven days to three weeks before they felt his intestines would function and Zack could eat. At three-day post op, Zack was looking hungry, had good bowel sounds, and clear liquid in the tube from his stomach. The surgeon said if it stayed this way, he could start eating as soon as possible.

An hour later, the rounds team of doctors came through with a totally different diagnosis. They felt it was way too early for Zack's body to be healed even if it looked like it was. They wanted to put in a central line to feed him for another week. Zack was in distress. He was sucking really hard and crying because he was hungry. It was hard to watch, but it meant he was healing. The parents' heads were spinning. Why another week? What did the surgeon see that these six doctors didn't? Who's right? Mom and Dad were just 21 years old. What do they do?

The nurse was not much help because she also thought it seemed way too soon after surgery for Zack to eat. Yet, he seemed ready--all the signs were there. Mom and Dad were confused. Who did they trust more at this time? Most of all, what was their gut telling them? I just sat with them and asked question after question to help them find their truth.

After about two hours of discussion, the rounds team came back to treat Zack as planned. Justin was tired, weak, and unsure of everything up until that moment. He stood up and said, "Don't touch my son. I want to talk to the surgeon." He demanded that the surgeon come. The surgeon came and assessed the situation, overrode the rounds' team discussion, looked at Mom and Dad and said "Let's feed him slow and see how it goes. As soon as he poops and he's stable, he goes home." Well, Zack ate, pooped within the next day, and was home that night.

What came over Justin? How did he and Janice get their answers? I just kept asking questions that made them think – it helped them process what was happening and made them more confident in what they knew. They found their own answers. That's why Justin was so strong at that moment—his gut took over.

They were two scared kids at the mercy of many credentials. Justin was heroic—and allowed himself to really understand what was right for Zack. I wasn't sure if either of them was going to step up, but the love for his son and the sight of more needles made Justin trust himself at the deepest level. The answers should have come from the doctor, but they didn't. In this case, they had to find them on their own. I nudged the process, but they needed to figure it out and they did. How's that for a package?

More answers came to me as well -- to observe how, even in such a large, respected medical center, care was as divided as Alternative and Western medicine. You will always have a difference of opinion in medicine, so your job as a patient is to know your body and be confident in yourself and ask a lot of questions. This is how you find your answers.

CHAPTER 20

Soul Mates

I WAS SEVENTEEN, out on my own, and working two jobs. I had just left home and an abusive relationship. I was just starting to learn what it meant to survive. Still, I knew if there were a way to figure out life, I would find it. I had a few friends I could call on for help, but I didn't know if they would be there for me during the toughest times.

I had met a guy at a few of the pit parties (you would meet at a secluded location and make a bonfire and have fun) that were the rage in my area back in the early 1980s. He and I worked for the same company, so we ran into each other frequently. The last thing on my mind was another relationship, but we stayed friendly. I'm not sure how it happened, but one day I ended up with my abusive ex- boyfriend. We were at a mall that was recently built in our area, and we had a huge disagreement. He left me stranded - no money, no car. I wasn't sure who to call for help.

I couldn't call home because I didn't live there anymore, and I didn't have close enough friends I could involve in this mess. I decided to go to the mall and find a pay phone to call this guy from work I hardly knew. Mind you, I didn't have his phone number, and I didn't even know his last name. I had no idea how I was going to find him.

I just knew that I had an overwhelming urge to go inside and call him. I walked through the mall entrance, and fifteen feet in, there he was, talking with a friend. I stopped in my tracks, not knowing what to say or even think. He saw I had been crying and asked if I was okay. Thirty-four years later, thirty years of marriage--I think I'm okay.

I've always felt that if something inside is urging me to pursue it, even though it doesn't make sense, I should explore it. If I had been overly rational that day, I would never have gone to the mall to call someone whose last name or phone number I didn't know. It just felt right.

Is he my soul mate? I say, "Yes." Are we perfect for each other in every way, see eye to eye on every subject, have all the same likes and dislikes? "Heck, no." What we do have is a partnership, and a meeting of the minds, sometimes with a lot of dialogue to get there but a meeting of the minds, nonetheless. Most importantly, we respect each other even though we don't always agree. We seldom argue because we're able to see each other's side of a situation. We're each allowed to have our own opinion and then come to a mutual agreement. It's about having respect for your partner, and not trying to control one another to make them think like you do.

Have you ever seen a married couple of 20, 30, 40 years? They often look alike, have the same walk, and even some of the same ailments. It's not unusual for them to have the same food likes, the same hobbies, and even the same friends. It's almost as if they're siblings, not a married couple. Why does this happen?

I want you to put both of your hands up in front of you. One hand is the husband's energy, and the other hand is the wife's energy -- or partner, or significant other. Now, slowly move your hands closer together. As they connect and, finally, one covers the other, this is how most married couples live. One person's energy completely meshes with his or her spouse's energy, so there's very little individual thought left. What I mean by that is not what you may think.

When two people live together, they tend to live in reaction. That is, each partner can anticipate how the other will respond to their actions in a given situation. So, they simply alter their behavior. Over time, the relationship takes on the sound of a well-rehearsed symphony – with each partner careful to play the right tune. In other words, both partners take on pretty defined roles in the relationship. But here's the problem. When you behave in anticipation of your spouse's reaction, instead of upsetting the situation or living in it to see what happens, it stops each person from living his or her truth. If one person in the relationship modifies their behavior to appease the other, then the stronger dominates the weaker. The weaker partner's energy is no longer theirs, it's their partner's.

Now, let's look at married couples who don't share any of the same characteristics. First, they don't look alike. They might have some mutual friends but also some of their own. They have separate hobbies and food likes and even very different philosophies on life. They can even agree to disagree. The hands don't cover each other. They stay independent of each other yet work together. Their energies are separate and blend when they choose to, but they're never influenced by the distortion of their partner's energy.

Which one has a true soul mate?

In my opinion, that would be the second couple. Most people want their partner to think like they think. I wish I had a dime for every conversation I've had with someone trying to make their partner think like they do. Don't get me wrong. There has to be a happy medium with the running of the household, raising kids, and so forth. But the automatic solution to a situation shouldn't be based on how the stronger partner views the world. Rather, the answer should come from both partners asking, "What's the right solution for <u>this</u> particular situation?" Who says your glasses see the world more clearly than your partner's?

I look at some of the topics people are trying to get their partners to embrace. Views on life, raising kids, managing money, and so forth. How many wives follow their husband's lead on these issues? Or, maybe it's the wife who's stronger, and the husband lets her choose everything.

Here's another possibility. What if the two of them have a difference of opinion, but instead of the usual weaker-stronger symphony, they decide to strike up a new chord. They discuss the situation openly, and without judgment. Perhaps, they come to the realization that neither is right. "We need to do more research and find a better answer than yours or mine." The same approach applies to money, food, health, and wellness.

Medical decisions are a big one. What if one partner decides to use more Alternative medicine and take control of their personal health care and wellness? Meanwhile, the other partner uses just Western medicine and its theories and chooses not to help themselves. I find this can turn a partnership toxic. Beliefs about medicine are equal to religious beliefs. When a partner goes one way and the spouse doesn't try to see the other's side, life becomes more challenging as a couple.

Wouldn't it be an interesting world if you could live in harmony with someone and respect their choices, even if you didn't share them? What would you gain? Perhaps more intellectual stimulation? Someone to challenge your thoughts and beliefs, and open you to new and enlightening ideas? In most relationships, there's always a submissive person to keep the peace. What do you think happens on a soul level if someone sacrifices themselves to keep the peace? In the beginning, it's not too bad. But after twenty or more years of playing this role, you now have two souls meshed into one. That means neither one heals. Plus, the sacrificing spouse is usually the one that gets sick because they have no strength in who they are. Hence, there's no strength to heal. What about when one of the partners die? How does the either one find peace if their energy is nestled together?

Let's look at teenagers. Why do they struggle so much with tangled energies and extreme relationships? Maybe, because it's easier to define themselves by someone else. Take your first love. You have to try it on, see how it fits. If you're strong in your intuition and make choices all the time, the love you are experiencing clouds the brain for a short time period, then you start to redefine yourself quickly. If you're not a strong person, you fall prey to using the other person's energy to make you feel whole. We have all seen that if one of them walks away, the weaker one crashes, is often abused, and can even become depressed or suicidal.

Think about when your kids start to question what you've taught them. Do you tell them <u>what</u> to think? Or, do you help them figure out what's best for them in each situation - even when it's not always what's best for you? Maybe if they made more choices as they were growing up, they wouldn't feel the need for someone else in their life to make them feel whole. The more you make decisions for yourself and learn what you want, the less dependent you are on others to fill those voids within you.

What about your own relationship with your spouse? What cues are your kids picking up? Are you demonstrating that you and your partner are soul mates or tangled energies? It saddened me many times when my daughter, Janice, was struggling with Justin. He came to me frequently because I talked to him and never took sides. Justin wanted to understand how to be an equal partner, not a controlling one. At times, he became very frustrated with me and screamed, "Nobody lives like you people do!" I thought, how sad is that? No drama, very little arguing. Everyone an equal in the household as far as having an opinion. Parents still directing the kids in a more positive direction. Each is respecting one another's space in conscious behavior. I really hope this is not as rare as Justin believed.

You see, Justin wanted to be the man of the house, but Janice never thought for a second that there was one person in charge - especially someone in charge of her when they would struggle. When they would argue, Janice would come and talk things over with me and found clarity because I didn't judge her, and she was able to make her own choices. She heard herself answer my questions and she came to her own realization about her relationship. She simply wanted more. It was a very challenging part of her journey, as well as mine. As a mom, I could feel her pain. However, if I talked negatively about Justin, it only would have pushed her closer to him. Instead, I just kept asking questions, letting her answer, and she realized she was giving herself the best advice she could receive.

One of the most valuable practices you can develop for your growth is to listen to yourself talk. Once you become aware of what's actually coming out of your mouth, you really start to learn who you are, and who you want to become. It's a wonderful gift to give yourself.

So, why are relationships so important to healing? It all goes back to balance. If you're mindful of balance with exercise, nutrition, rest, and so forth but your relationship is still taxing your energy, then you're still out of balance. And you won't be able to heal.

I've watched a lot of women with cancer not take the proper time for themselves. They continue to take care of everyone and everything in the household. Somehow, they're able to keep up with their treatments and still serve their family. In reality, they're exhausted -- and they're <u>not</u> healing. They tell me, "My family can't see that I'm tired, and nobody helps unless I ask, so it's easier just to do things myself." My reply? "If you don't ask, and it's all still getting done, how do they know it's a problem for you? You're still living in the same pattern that got you here."

When is it her time to heal? Why doesn't her family see her struggle? Are they really that blind? Did she train them a long time ago, so they have no idea what she wants or needs, or is she that good at pushing herself beyond her limits and not showing weakness?

The risk of living in reactionary relationships, whether it's marriage or with your children, is when you choose to change. When you decide to change your pattern of behavior, your established M.O., make no mistake, it will upset the dynamics in the household. It has to. The person healing will see the need for change, but will anyone else? Usually, the one trying to change things is the one that is not feeling well and needs help. That means the shift in responsibility will go on to others who do not want the extra work, making it hard for the sick person to create the change. This limits their healing potential.

When trying to heal ourselves and relationships, I find the biggest obstacle stems from what I call societal blueprints - patterns of behaviors you pick up from society. Take life sixty years ago, when Mom stayed home and raised the family. Lots of us grew up watching those behaviors. Mom took care of everything and Dad went to work. Today, it's more likely that both partners' work. Problems surface when Dad still lives like his dad did, and Mom still lives like her mom. It's an unfair balance. I see the struggles of a lot of women. It's a classic reactionary situation. She gets upset, yells, but nobody listens. He doesn't see the problem because his behavior is all reaction to what he saw his dad do. Neither partner has actually observed themselves to see how they react, how they behave, and how the house is really run. They just get up every day and continue on the treadmill of dysfunction. What if they sat with a spreadsheet and mapped it all out: what it takes to run the house, who does what and who takes time for themselves and takes care of themselves. Both would probably be shocked. But now you are aware of how things really are not as each individual sees them, and now change can occur.

Now, take a look at your partner and ask yourself, "Why am I here? Why do I love him/her? Does my relationship make me strong or weaken my being? Do I treat my partner as an equal, or do I try to get them to think like me? If they don't share my opinion, do I see why they don't, or do I block it out because it's easier?"

Are you walking the path of least resistance or trying to learn about yourself?

If you share the same opinion, is it because you both think the same? Or is one person simply trying to appease the other? If your husband/wife is trying to appease you, ask yourself why.

Sometimes, a partner's difference of opinion is the best teacher. Think about it. If they see a situation differently, then they just showed you another way to look at life – and maybe offered you some clarity and even more possibilities in your healing.

Hey, maybe, that's what love is.

The Body Within

CHAPTER 21

Healing Others While Healing Yourself

I WAS SITTING IN THE corner of my treatment room with a client on the table. The lights were very dim, and the room was very quiet. I was discussing the last couple of sessions -- how her reluctance to change and her unwillingness to abandon the negative path she'd chosen is suffocating her energy.

Why her? Theresa spent many years as a Shaman-in-training, she has taken courses and learned how to become a Shaman from a classroom. Shamanism is a life's work of training the mind, body, and soul. Traditional Shamans were tested for strength and endurance for how much they could tolerate in all three areas of Mind, Body, and Soul from their early childhood to adulthood. Most people have no understanding of what that means. Even from a tribal standpoint, today there are very few true Shamans who understand the depth of knowledge and commitment required to do the healing work they do. You may <u>think</u> that you know something is hard, but becoming a Shaman is as difficult as becoming a Navy Seal. There's a reason there are so few of those too.

Theresa had gone to all the Shaman classes and worked with a master, performing countless healings on people. She would be in the room with the Master Teacher, learning his trade, which dealt with negative energies and emotional issues of all kinds.

Theresa's biggest mistake, her weakness, was that she approached learning Shamanism as if she were in a typical classroom. But to be a Shaman is to commit to a life, not a lifestyle. Theresa saw Shamanism the way she wanted it to be but never incorporated it into her own healing. This disconnect was overtaking her in an extremely negative way.

The critical piece Theresa missed was that she was supposed to heal with each one of her clients. Theresa didn't understand that she was not the healer, but that her role was to be a facilitator of their healing – the facilitator of the joint power and strength she and her client had together.

So, how can you heal yourself while healing others and why do you want to? It's actually easier than you might think, easier than being ashamed Whenever you're having a conversation with someone and they seem to be struggling with life, that's your cue to take a step back and really look at who they are instead of blurting out advice you think they should take. What do you know about them, and why they think and choose the things they do? How did they grow up, where do they live, what is their faith, are they male or female, how old are they, what is their schooling? All of these things define how they see life and how they make choices. Once you're able to see them for who they really are, you can offer advice. Or better yet, ask them questions so they can give themselves advice. As soon as you go to that level inside yourself to help others, you can see the same possibilities in your life. You can see all the things in your life that affect your own choices. Theresa overlooked that part that I call the mirror of healing.

Many female clients my age come through my office and most are married to men of the same generation and grew up in the same area as my husband. Yes, people from the same generation tend to have a lot of the same thoughts and actions, unless they've been awake enough to break patterns and think completely for themselves.

I could put my husband and at least four of my friends' husbands in a room, present a scenario, and they all responded similarly, if not the same. It's an energy imprint of a generation. Take some time to observe your parents and others their age, along with people your age, and their kids and friends. Sure, there may be some independent thinkers in the mix, but most carry a lot of the same thoughts and theories. Blueprints are not only family-generated but society- generated also. This will help you not only see yourself clearer but also help you when you are helping others. This will help you understand advice is less valuable than questions. Questions always create thought, thought breaks patterns.

How do I heal alongside my clients? I talk with them about issues they have with their spouses. I mirror my own relationship with my husband. At that moment, I make a choice to reflect on how we live and how we handle similar issues. Do we bury them, or do we discuss them and try to solve them? Every time you observe or talk with someone, it gives you an opportunity to see yourself, for better or worse. It helps you see how far you've come or how far you still have to go. Mirroring also shows you how many more tools you have than them, or how much more aware of life you are. Just as valuable, sometimes you see how much more aware of life they are than you are.

Perhaps our greatest learning opportunity occurs when you reach out to help someone. You may give them what you believe is the answer to their problem. However, they can't see that it's a realistic answer. You wonder why can't they see it? Then you realize there's just no way they will make the changes you're suggesting. This creates a dilemma for you. You may ask yourself, "Why can't they see that all they have to do is make this one change, and their life will improve?" It's hard for you to process their lack of clarity. When this happens -- and it will again and again - it should motivate you to look in the mirror. Ask yourself, "Do I see reality clearly? Or is this scenario a healing tool coming to me so that I can see my own reflection? Do I need to make changes and can't or won't?" Ask yourself why. Then take it one step further to see if they make the change you are suggesting. Do they have the support or resources to be able to find peace in making that change? Most times they don't. It's too much for them even to consider. Maybe baby-steps in your advice might be a better fit.

Here's an example of baby-steps. One day, a client Rob in his late 60s, with poor health habits, and a hard worker, told me about a conversation he had with his brother regarding nutrition and exercise. Rob was furious because he felt that all his brother had to do was take his advice and his life would change for the better. Rob kept asking me, "Why won't he listen?" After a few minutes of Rob raising his blood pressure recounting this conversation with his brother, I busted out laughing. Rob looked at me, stunned. I said to him, "What you told your brother was word for word what I've been telling you for two years. Apparently, you really were listening."

After a few minutes, Rob did better than just see the irony, he saw the clarity. He realized how overwhelmed his wife and everyone around him had been by him and his choices, and how ignoring his health was not doing him a service at all. Did he change his habits at that moment? No, but now he knows he has them. Baby steps.

I was talking to yet another person about her struggles with a spouse, how the spouse was very overweight because of poor diet and lack of exercise. She couldn't understand why he wouldn't help himself. Again, I took a step back and asked her, "What did you have for breakfast and when was the last time you exercised?" She replied, "But I'm not overweight." To which I responded, "You're not healthy either. You just have a better metabolism."

The message? Pay close attention to your actions with your kids, spouse, parents, and take some time to reflect. Is it really about them? Or are you trying to change them to make them who you want them to be, instead of letting them be who they are? Or is it possible you're trying to fix yourself by fixing them?

I'll say it again – mirror, mirror, mirror. Whenever you're dispensing advice in an effort to help others, your words will always benefit you if you actually listen to what you're saying.

CHAPTER 22

Balance Breeds Peace

EIGHT-YEAR-OLD ZACK went to Lacrosse camp for a week. On day two, he came over for a visit and said "Grammy, look when I bend and scoop the ball on my left side, I can go down this far, but when I bend and scoop on the right side, I can only bend half-way down. My belly scar is stopping me from bending and is making my knee act funny. Can you help me fix it, please?"

Small for his age, athletic, smart open minded and fun, he had learned how to assess his own issues with his body early on. This is excellent, and if an eight-year-old can do it, so can you.

Grant is a sixteen-year-old hockey player. While playing in a particularly close game, he took a hit to his hips and his mother brought him in. He told me that when he closes his eyes and focuses, he can see his left hip and the ligaments are pulling the joint, so it does not look straight. He tried to stretch out of it, but the only thing that seems to help is massaging the area. However, it does not seem to release it fully. He had talked to the athletic trainer and he said it was fine, but grant knew it was not. He wanted help in correcting it.

Jenny, a nineteen-year-old college student, who has been suffering from chronic pain in her muscles and has been working on healing herself for about a year. After doing yoga, she said she could feel a lot of tension around her left lower ribs and when she closed her eyes, she could see that the energy was not connected to the rest of her midsection. It was like she was missing part of her side. She thinks it's because she had mono and remembered how much it had hurt at the time. She felt that if we corrected it, she would be able to get deeper into her stretching and it would help her heal.

Stanley is a sixty-five-year-old man who suffered many physical injuries in his life and was working to get his body back. Tall and muscular, retired from his career as an engineer, he wanted more function and no pain in his body. He came in for one of his sessions and said he had been having dreams about one of his accidents and felt he needed to revisit and clear the energy from it to heal.

Margie is a forty-five-year-old woman with breast cancer and during her chemo treatments, she told me she took a deep breath and brought white light all the healing powers of the chemo in, and exhaled negative energy with the intent to get rid of any of the side effects of the chemo. She said other patients thought she was crazy until they saw she was not getting sick and worn out. I asked her where she read to do this and she said just came to her, and it felt right.

So many stories, so little time. Just know, the more balanced and aware you become, the more tools you will have to be your own healer. Medicines, supplements, exercise, meditations, yoga, and so forth are all just a piece of the puzzle. You, my friend, are the key to making all those tools work for you. Here's one more story to help you understand how much personal power you have and how you owe it to yourself to at least try to tap into a small piece of it.

Lucille was 85 years old. She'd had a wonderful life – a loving husband and seven amazing children. A true matriarch, she lived her life and her truth to the max. She had her faith, but she didn't get caught up in the rules or the politics. She used her faith as a guide to help her find her meaning. Now the years were catching up with her. Lucille was slowing down, losing her health, and her heart wasn't as strong. Her husband had died two years prior.

Lucille was still living alone, going out with friends, line dancing once a week, and living a productive, whole life. One day, she had a talk with her son and said, "I just want to let you know that I'm good. I've had a great life, and I'm tired. I just want to be with your dad." Two weeks later, she went to the doctor. Her heart had kept her going as long as it could, and now it could no longer sustain her. It was quickly breaking down. Lucille was really okay with it. Her children were adjusting but also deeply saddened.

In less than ten days, Lucille was in her home in her own bed with family surrounding her. She was weak and falling in and out of sleep. Early in the evening, she woke up and asked, "What time is it?" Lucille's daughters replied, "Mom, it's 6:00 PM." Lucille looked at them, surprised, and said, "Oh my, I've missed my glass of wine before dinner." What were the girls to do? They broke open a bottle of wine, poured everyone a glass, and toasted Mom. Lucille took a few sips and fell back asleep. She died just moments later.

Lucille was the mom of a very dear friend. She was also the mom of Paul in Chapter 18 who came to peace with his dad's death by writing the Top 10 list. Because of the changes Paul made with his dad's dying, these changed helped him, his mother, and his family adopts a clearer vision of death. In turn, this clarity helped their mom die peacefully. As Paul made choices to listen and observe, he also made choices to change himself and his beliefs. The learning he gained through his parents' deaths raised his energy vibration, which will help him and his children throughout their lives. A single shift of awareness in one person can truly change the outcome for many.

In closing, I urge you to remember all the tools you have accumulated throughout your reading. Use them on yourself daily and really start to open yourself and others to a new and infinite way of thinking. There are lots of people in the world with personal agendas -- to save the Earth, counteract global warming, feed the hungry, and so forth. My agenda is to get you to look inside yourself. To view yourself and others, and to see where your agenda and your reality lie. Really start to embrace *The Body Within*. Embrace the messages coming your way.   Know that life is an amazing journey filled with choices, and that there are infinite possibilities available to you for healing. You just need to start to open up to the possibility that you are our own healer and the medicine is just a tool.

As you look around and see the imbalanced energy in the world around you, know that:

CHAOS BREEDS CHAOS.
BALANCE BREEDS PEACE.

Know that bringing balance into your life creates: Peace
in who you are.
Peace in how you live.
Peace when it's time to die.

Here's to you!

May you become your own healer and live a more balanced and peaceful life, age gracefully and leave in a balanced, peaceful way. You are your answer.

Marie ☺

NOTES

NOTES

Marie Knoetig

NOTES

Marie Knoetig

Marie Knoetig

Made in the USA
Monee, IL
14 November 2020